FACE YOUR NEXT INTERVIEW
– WITH CONFIDENCE

By the same author:

Sharpen Up Your Interviewing (Mercury Books, 1991)

FACE YOUR NEXT INTERVIEW – WITH CONFIDENCE

JACK GRATUS

MERCURY

First published in 1992
by Mercury Books
Gold Arrow Publications Limited,
862 Garratt Lane, London SW17 0NB

Set in Sabon by Phoenix Photosetting
Printed and bound in Great Britain by
Mackays of Chatham PLC, Chatham, Kent

British Library Cataloguing in Publication Data is available

ISBN 1–85251–121–4

CONTENTS

CONTENTS

CONTENTS

INTRODUCTION

The purpose of this book

'I hate interviews. It's like going to the dentist – being strapped in a chair and drilled.'

'The only part of the interview I enjoy is the relief when it's over.'

'Only interviewers get any fun out of interviews because they can push their weight around and you can't do anything about it.'

Interviews are most people's idea of hell. For managers, conducting an interview is only marginally more pleasant than attending one. Yet they are at the core of most of our lives – not only in business, but in our other day-to-day activities. We cannot get a job without the interview; nor a promotion or rise. We cannot obtain a mortgage or a bank overdraft. And try telling a doctor, or a lawyer, our physical, or legal, problem if they do not ask the appropriate questions.

Perhaps it is because we have such unpleasant memories of early meetings with headteachers and the other figures of authority that dogged our childhood that we take with us into adulthood our fear and loathing of the interview. Perhaps it is because, so often, so much depends on our doing well at the interview that we imbue it with almost mystical significance – like those formidable tests the warriors and heroes of mythology were always being subjected to.

Another reason interviews hold terror for so many of us is that they represent the great unknown. We will be spending time with complete strangers who may ask us difficult questions, the answers to which we do not know, and we will be exposed to them for our ignorance. What is needed, therefore, is a way of dealing with the unknown, of countering it with a system that, properly applied, will help to overcome practically any obstacle that may be encountered.

Which is where the PQRSTU System comes in. By reducing the confusing and threatening elements of the interview to a basic system, you should be able to handle any kind of interview that comes your way with the kind of confidence that gets you the job, the promotion, the rise, the mortgage, or puts your case across to the media. Master the system and you will have no real difficulty with any future interviews, since it will provide you with a thorough understanding of the basic elements of interviewing, no matter what the purpose or subject matter.

In addition, by familiarising yourself with the PQRSTU System, you will acquire:

- greater confidence to deal with other situations such as meetings and negotiations
- greater ability to convince others of your skills and achievements
- greater control over yourself and your material

A word of caution, though. No book on interviewing (or any other management skill, for that matter), irrespective of how excellently written and comprehensive, can beat experience. The more interviews you attend, the better you will get at them – provided, or course, you evaluate each interview calmly and objectively after it is finished, because it is from your mistakes as well as your successes that you learn to improve your skills as an interviewee.

Who is the book aimed at?

Anyone going for a new job, or to an appraisal interview where promotion or a rise could be at stake, or worse, a chewing out. It is also aimed at executives whose work requires them to attend press conferences at which their firm's latest product is about to be launched, and at people such as writers, artists, musicians, craftsmen and women who need to sell themselves in order to sell their products. It should also help the self-employed in every sphere to get more business.

I hear your objections: isn't every interview different? How can you cover all situations in one book? The answer is that, by adopting a systematic rather than a haphazard approach, you will be in a far better position to handle to your own satisfaction *any* interview you may be required to attend.

Interviews are a two-way process. You are not a passive victim, dragged in off the street to be subjected to aggressive, probing questions by a hostile stranger. You are a sentient, intelligent human being with something to say for yourself and it is in your power to make the points you want to make and to influence the outcome of every interview which your work and your domestic life require you to attend.

Two more points to remember: first, although in retrospect they may seem interminable, few interviews last more than an hour, so they take up only a small fraction of your life; and second, many interviewers find interviewing just as traumatic as interviewees. If, therefore, you are equipped with greater understanding of how the process works, you will have a considerable advantage.

How this book is arranged

In Part One, the PQRSTU System is analysed in detail, showing its applicability and relevance to all kinds of interview. In Part Two, the PQRSTU System is applied to media interviews and to the most common and the most demanding of all interviews, recruitment, and this is done by way of brief, concise checklists. Readers whose next job interview is about to take place are recommended to read through these before the full exposition of the PQRSTU System in Part One.

What is an interview?

In my reading on the subject I have come across widely varying definitions of the interview, some in direct contradiction to others. Writers compare them to conversations, to games, and to theatrical performances, and, as anyone who has been to an interview will confirm, they do incorporate all those elements plus a few more.

There are some essential elements common to all. For an interview to work, there must be:

- at least two participants
- one who 'sets the agenda' and controls the proceedings by asking the questions
- that the other answers
- for a particular purpose
- which is known to both

To this list can be added the point that interviews are, in general, deliberately set up, with all the consequences this implies. Some, of course, are apparently impromptu, as when one executive meets another in the company car-park or the office corridor, but even these, if analysed, would probably turn out to be rather less spontaneous than might at first appear. One of the participants has probably been planning it for some time and may even have been lying in wait for the other, so as to ambush them with their questions before the other has had time to prepare a defence. Even the supposedly idle 'chat' between senior manager and junior executive may be based on question and answer that the latter will become aware of only after it is all over.

The idea that interviews are 'conversations' is a popular misconception. Though the best interviews are frequently conversational in tone, they are usually quite strictly controlled — by the interviewers if they are on top of their material, by the interviewees if they are sufficiently assertive and well-prepared. Good conversations should have no particular purpose, but are enjoyed by the participants merely for the sake of exchanging views. Interviews, however, should always have a purpose, and both participants should be aware of this before and during the interviews. If they are not purposeful, or if the purpose is not shared by both participants, the interviews will be ineffective.

Game-playing and role-playing are also part of every interview. Some interviewers, otherwise mild-mannered and thoughtful, suddenly become tyrants when faced by submissive and frightened interviewees. Interviewees equally may be playing that role, hoping that by appearing terrified the interviewers will be sympathetic towards them and give them an easier time.

One game interviewers like to play is 'hide the meaning'. This is when they ask questions that appear to have one purpose but, in fact, mean something completely different. For instance, when the interviewer asks, 'What particular problems have you had to deal with in your present job?' she really means, 'I would like to know how you get on with your boss or your colleagues.' Similarly, when the interviewee answers, 'All things considered, we've had a pretty good relationship,' he probably means, 'Considering that I've made one hell of a mess of my job, they've treated me quite well.'

When both participants have facts and feelings they wish to hide they may 'play' the interview like a card game. A candidate in a recruitment interview, for example, may have an episode in his life which he would rather the recruiter knew nothing of — a spell of unemployment, or being fired for incompetence, for instance. Equally, the interviewer might prefer it if the candidate did not know that, due to poor management, the company had recently gone through half-a-dozen employees in the post for which the candidate is applying. The result is that, being more concerned to conceal than reveal the true positions, both participants hold their cards so close to their respective chests that their game never reaches a wholly satisfactory conclusion. The fact remains that the more interviews resemble games than searching and honest exchanges, the less useful information will pass, which means that neither participant can make effective decisions based on what they have learnt.

Another game interviews have been rightly likened to, but in a more positive sense, is tennis. In the ideal open, unstructured interview, the subject matter is lobbed back and forth from interviewer to interviewee, with both giving their full effort to keeping the action lively and enjoyable. The only difference is that in tennis the aim of each player is to win; in interviewing the aim should be that they both win, or, in other words, that they both come away with a sense of having achieved something worthwhile.

In some respects, interviews resemble marriage. Just as every newlywed has a different idea of what constitutes a good marriage, and what to expect from one, so every interviewer and interviewee goes into the interview not knowing how it is going to turn out, whether they will 'click' or whether they will get on each other's nerves and be only too happy to bring the proceedings to a swift and painless end.

Whatever they may be compared to, interviews are, essentially, unnatural and contrived, and it is virtually impossible for the participants to behave as they would in normal encounters. In my own interviewing seminars I work with a group of executives who know each other well, having spent much of their working lives together, but the instant I place them in role-playing situations where they have to interview each other about subjects outside of their work, they become virtual strangers to each other, as self-conscious as if they had never met before. And when, as a journalist, I had to interview my own friends for a magazine feature, I found that, as soon as I started asking questions, they assumed the role of strangers, and facts about their personal lives that hitherto they had freely discussed with me became closely guarded secrets.

The unnaturalness of interviews is exacerbated by the many contradictions and paradoxes with which they are surrounded. For example, while pretending to conduct an informal and open discussion, with each participant playing an equal role, interviewers are actually in control of the process from start to finish. There is also the pretence that they are objective and without prejudice, whereas, at recruitment interviews especially, many interviewers make up their minds about a candidate within the first five minutes and spend the rest of the time looking for details that will confirm their decision.

Interviewees, as we shall discuss in greater detail later, are placed in particularly awkward 'no-win situations'. They are expected, and often encouraged, to talk, but if they talk too much, interviewers will condemn them for it. Interviewees are expected to assert themselves, but only up to a point. If they go a little too far, they are regarded as too pushy. And just as interviewers are supposed to be open and honest, but frequently are neither, so, too, are interviewees, who have far more to lose if they behave as they are expected to do.

Unnatural, contrived and potentially dishonest? You may well ask what is the point of interviews, and in one area particularly – staff recruitment – there is a growing body of opinion that at best they are unreliable, at worst a waste of time and money, because many candidates chosen through interview turn out not to be suitable. Nevertheless, interviewing is a vital part of management, and no one has yet come up with a viable alternative. What is more, in the hands of competent, experienced, well-trained interviewers, they are a very effective management tool.

It is, however, interesting that while companies may spend money and time training their executives to conduct interviews, they never, to my knowledge, spend a penny training staff as interviewees. Yet, were they to do so, they might find the results very satisfactory, because the interviews themselves would be far more fulfilling, with both participants giving and expecting their best, and the results would be much more reliable.

The reason that companies do not train interviewees is, of course, obvious. Interviewees who know how an interview works, who have developed insight into what occurs between the two participants, will not be passive victims, but will be pro-active participants who will make sure that they achieve their purpose, and will be equipped to give as good as they get. It is my hope and expectation that, after reading this book, you will be in such a position.

Types of interview and interviewer

When, as an applicant for a job, you are invited to attend an interview, you usually have no idea what kind of interview it is going to be. Will it be formal or informal, structured or unstructured? Is there a difference, and can you prepare yourself if you do not know what that difference is?

Similar questions may be asked about interviews for other purposes. An appraisal interview may be formal and rigidly conducted, where the interviewee has little room to manoeuvre, or it might be 'conversational', with lots of emphasis on the interviewee's feelings. Only media interviews are invariably unstructured – or, at least, appear to be, because some journalists, either for lack of time or lack of confidence prepare themselves by learning a set of questions by heart, which they stick to no matter what happens.

There are basically two main types of interview – the structured and unstructured. Briefly, the structured interview follows a set pattern from start to finish, and although an interviewer asks the questions, from the interviewee's point of view such interviews are no more interesting or enjoyable than filling in a long questionnaire. In these interviews, not only the questions, but to some extent the answers – or choice of answers – have been formulated in advance. The advantage of structured interviews, according to their proponents, is that they are more objective, and their results can be more easily and accurately predicted. It is for this last reason that they are favoured by personnel departments of many big corporations which are regularly required to select large numbers of new staff.

Market research and opinion poll interviews are mainly of the structured type, and structured interviews are also used to good effect by other professions, such as the medical profession for diagnostic purposes. Recently, attending a clinic for my regular health check, I sat with an interactive computer which asked me many intimate questions about my health and my lifestyle, and all I was required to do was press my finger on what I thought was the right answer. By the end of half an hour, it knew more about me and my health than the doctor I have consulted for years.

The main disadvantage of the structured interview is that no real rapport can be established between the participants. Impressed though I was by my diagnostic computer, I did not warm to it in any way, nor, I presume, it to me. Interviewers' prejudices and biases may be minimised, but so, too, will their experience as interviewers and judges of character.

Unstructured interviews simulate conversations, but, as we have seen, in reality they are controlled by the interviewers. At their best they permit a full and open exchange of views and feelings, on the strength of which effective decisions can be made and actions taken for the benefit of both. But in the hands of untrained and incompetent interviewers (regrettably, the majority), they may do more harm than good. They meander pointlessly; they lack purpose and achieve nothing. Potentially ideal employees are turned away in favour of candidates who appeal to interviewers for reasons other than their suitability. Appraisal interviews, instead of motivating employees, can end with employees threatening to find new jobs. Media interviews can degenerate into arguments or informal chats, and nothing useful is achieved. The list of potential disasters is endless.

Nonetheless, in spite of their drawbacks, it is with unstructured interviews that I am mainly concerned in this book, because they are still the most common and, more important, interviewees have the opportunity to make a positive contribution to their development and outcome.

As we shall see, interviewers adopt a wide variety of styles.

At one extreme there are those whose interviews follow a strict plan and who regard themselves more as interrogators. They ask limiting questions requiring mainly 'Yes' or 'No' answers, and they control the pace and the timing, interrupting interviewees when they have the information they want. They also talk at least as much as the interviewees. With such interviewers you have very little room for manoeuvre; however, with good planning, patience and persistence, you may still be able to influence the outcome of such interviews in your own favour.

At the other extreme there are those interviewers who, by asking open questions and talking as little as possible, give interviewees the freedom to express their thoughts and feelings. To make the best use of such an interview, you still need to do some preparation, as well as taking an active role in defining its purpose and limiting its scope, otherwise the interview may go out of control and be a waste of time.

The majority of interviews lie somewhere between these two extremes. They are neither interrogations nor are they open-ended counselling sessions, but are a two-way process of communication in which both parties are receivers and senders of information. Some degree of equality between the participants is not only desirable, but is essential. Control does not lie solely in the hands of interviewers, and questions can be asked by interviewees, who will probably do at least 80 per cent of the talking. Though there may be a plan of sorts, interviewers in these essentially unstructured interviews are flexible enough to alter it if circumstances demand. Interviewees, if they have mastered the PQRSTU System, should be able to make the most of themselves and secure the results they wish.

Whatever the type of interview or interviewer, you are entitled to be treated in a manner that I have set down as:

The Interviewees' Charter

All interviewees should be

10

- taken seriously
- treated with dignity
- given respect as another human being
- challenged by interesting, thought-provoking questions so that they can give the most interesting, thought-provoking responses
- given adequate time to prepare
- given adequate time to answer the questions
- left with their self-esteem intact, no matter what the circumstances

How to influence the interview

The idea that interviewees, by their very nature, have to be passive victims is, I believe, a mistaken one. Successful interviewees – and by that I mean those who achieve what they set out to do, be it to get the offer of a job, the promotion, or the opportunity to state their case – are those who *take charge*, not necessarily in the sense that they take over the interview and run it as they please, because then the interviewer has lost all control, but that they are, as far as the rules of interviewing permit, equal partners in the endeavour.

In my earlier book, *Sharpen Up Your Interviewing* (Mercury Books, 1991), I advised interviewers that the focus of their attention should be their interviewees. I summed up the point by saying that the interview belongs to the interviewee. I shall be developing this theme further and showing how you, the interviewee, can ensure that you make the very most of the attention that is given to you by the interviewer. I realise how difficult this must seem if you are about to face an interviewer who has spent years conducting interviews and who has the reputation of destroying the self-esteem of many a timid and defenceless interviewee. But I would not have written this book unless I fervently believed that you can learn enough about interviews to make sure that, in future, your interviews go more or less where you would like them to go.

Interviewers usually call the shots. The interview takes place in their office and at their convenience. They control the agenda, since it is their questions that lay down what subjects are going to be discussed, and in what order. They also establish the timing and the pace, and when they wish to end it, they can. As an interviewee, your ability to influence the interview depends partly on yourself, and partly on the style of interviewing adopted by the interviewer. The single purpose that informs the PQRSTU System – and gives it its strength – is that it is a means whereby you, the interviewee, can establish and maintain some semblance of equality in what is essentially an unequal relationship.

PART ONE
THE PQRSTU SYSTEM

1

PREPARATION

WHY PREPARE YOURSELF?

The rule that applies to all interviews is: *expect the unexpected*.

You can never know what kind of interview you are going to have, but it is as well to remember that, very often, interviewers are no better trained at the craft of interviewing than you are at being interviewed. They may have had more experience, though even this is not guaranteed, but they are likely to be as uncomfortable as you are. The exceptions are personnel officers and staff recruitment interviewers (usually the same people) working for large companies, who are continually interviewing new staff or conducting appraisals for their employers. They are properly trained and are usually well briefed and prepared. Their skills make your task as interviewee more demanding, but they also allow you more chance to shine, because practised interviewers know how to encourage you to give full replies to their questions.

Regrettably, even in large personnel departments of major organisations, good interviewers are rather less the rule than the exception, and in smaller companies most executives who have to conduct interviews have had little or no training. The worst believe they need none. 'Anyone can do it,' is the phrase I have sometimes heard from executives who come to me for training, and who usually turn out to be both inadequate as human beings and incompetent as interviewers.

What has been said about executives applies equally to

journalists. Few of them have had any training, and fewer still have the time or inclination to make proper preparations. This means that, on the one hand, the task of the interviewees is made more difficult because they have to work harder to keep the interview focused on them, while, on the other hand, it is easier for them to control the proceedings without, of course, appearing to do so.

However good or bad the interviewers you meet are, it is essential that you are properly prepared. The worse the interviewer, in fact, the better prepared you have to be if you want to achieve anything from the interview. Good preparation means far more than just being able to answer questions, though that, of course, is an essential part of it. It means knowing what you want to get out of the interview, and how to go about getting it. With good preparation comes confidence, and with confidence comes the self-assurance necessary to achieve your objectives, whatever they may be. Skimp on preparation and you are seriously crippling your chances of being made an offer of the job you are after, getting the rise or promotion you want and deserve, or making the right kind of impact on the media.

HOW TO PREPARE YOURSELF

Many years ago when the great singer and entertainer Sammy Davis Jr was at the height of his career, he was asked by a journalist how he kept in the public eye. His reply was. 'The moment I leave my house in the morning, I am "on", Daddy, I'm "on"!' He meant by this that to make an impact, he had to put his heart and mind to it. To a lesser degree, this is what happens when you go to your interview. You are putting yourself forward to be noticed and, therefore, the image you present to the interviewer as well as the information you wish to convey must be carefully thought out in advance, without actually seeming to be.

This takes preparation which, in turn, takes time and planning. These are the steps to follow to make sure that you will be seen by the interviewer in the way you intend:

Step 1: Decide whether or not you want to be interviewed.
Step 2: Find out as much as you can about the interview.
Step 3: Find out about yourself.
Step 4: Decide what points you want to get across.
Step 5: Imagine six questions you most dread being asked, and work out the answers.

Step 1

Do you or do you not want to be interviewed? You may not, of course, have any choice in the matter, if, say, you are summoned to an appraisal interview by your boss. But for most other interviews, you can decide whether or not you wish to be interviewed. Appearing before the media, for example, is seldom compulsory and, unless it is part of your job as a press officer, you can always say 'No' to a journalist seeking to interview you.

In order to reach a decision, you should ask yourself what good the interview will do you. 'Is this a job I really want?' would be a valid question for a candidate to ask before accepting an invitation to a recruitment interview. 'Will it do me or my firm any good if I agree to speak to the press or go on a radio or television programme?' It is said that all publicity is good publicity, But this is not necessarily the case. Launching a product or service before all the problems have been sorted out may set back its reception beyond recovery; in which case, you should be brave enough to decline.

Only agree to be interviewed if, having thought through all the consequences, you decide that, on balance it would be advantageous to do so.

Step 2

Find out as much as you can about the interview, in particular:

- when it will take place
- where it will take place
- who will interview you
- how you get there
- whether your travel expenses will be paid
- why you are being interviewed, rather than someone else in your organisation
- what the interview is going to be about
- what questions you are likely to be asked

For obvious reasons, the last point may be the most difficult to find out about. Few journalists care to give away the precise details of their interview, because it spoils the spontaneity of the exchange. You have to be either a leading politician or a famous celebrity to get away with that one, though increasingly the public relations departments of major corporations are demanding that journalists send them a list of questions before they allow any of their executives to speak to the press.

Job hunters will find it virtually impossible to obtain answers to all but the first five questions. Nevertheless, if you are going after a job, it is essential that you obtain satisfactory answers to those questions before you attend the interview. Determined though you may be to get the job, you should avoid wasting time and energy chasing after interviews that are unlikely to yield positive results. Doing so is one of the surest ways to undermine your self-esteem, a commodity that is usually in short supply, particularly if you are unemployed.

In addition to those questions, candidates for jobs should also obtain details of the company or organisation as well as of the job for which they are applying. Brochures, company reports, indeed anything that will give you more information about the organisation, will give you a much better idea of what to expect when you go to the interview, as well as

18

showing the recruiter that you are serious about your application.

Step 3

Having obtained all the information you can about the interviewer and the nature of the interview, your next step is to find out about yourself. This idea may seem a little strange – after all, if you do not already know yourself, who does? – but the reasons for doing so are perfectly sound. When you go to a recruitment interview, or when you are selling your own or your company's products, you need to stand out from the others. Recruiters and journalists see many interviewees in the course of their working day; the ones they remember are those who strike them as being different and having something interesting to say. You do not want to make your mark by displays of bizarre behaviour (unless, of course, you are a professional entertainer where that may be a good way of attracting attention) but by the uniqueness of your personality.

However, before you can do that, you have to know who you are and what makes you different from others. This requires, you will be pleased to learn, not a session with a psychiatrist, but rather some constructive self-appraisal, which is not as easy to do as it may at first seem.

One of the greatest barriers to effective self-presentation is fear. Most of us, when we have to go in front of strangers, fear that we are being closely observed, studied and judged. Those who suffer low self-esteem also believe that they fail to pass the test. It is true that in interviews there is always a certain amount of judging, and interviewers are usually more interested in how we look and behave than what we have to say, but dwelling on this does not improve our performance. On the contrary, it makes it worse.

The trick, if you can call it that, is to think outwards, not inwards; to concentrate, not on ourselves, but on the interviewer and the questions put to us. However, to do that requires that we feel comfortable with ourselves by accepting ourselves as we are, warts and all. Except that the warts should never be allowed to dominate our self-view; the self-appraisal I am recommending should always be conducted in a positive spirit.

None of us is perfect, and we all have done things in our lives that we are not proud of, but we cannot turn the clock back to change them. Our weaknesses are just as valid a part of us as our strengths, and though we choose not to flaunt them, we should not attempt to hide them from ourselves – that way, they merely eat away at us in the form of shame or remorse, which can be more destructive to our self-esteem than the severest of criticism from others.

The most practical way to assess yourself positively is to make a list of all your accomplishments, not merely the major achievements in your life, but *everything* you have done that other people should know about. It is extraordinary how difficult many people find this to do. Perhaps it is because we are brought up to believe that talking about ourselves and our successes is boasting, so we tend to discount or play down our achievements. When we go through our careers we leave out items which we consider of little importance but which, if properly presented, would give the outside world a far more complete picture of what we have done and are capable of doing. The rule is: *small details add up*.

Your weaknesses, too, should go down on a list – only here, we should also try to find a positive way of presenting them. So, instead of listing, say, impatience as a failing, we might put down, 'over-eager to get things done'. This is not hiding from the truth. On the contrary, it is putting an affirmative interpretation on negative characteristics, which is a very different thing. It is neither in our own interest nor in the interests of those with whom we have to deal that they are privy to our self-doubts. Unless these affect their business, they are *not* their business.

Listing strengths and weaknesses works equally well with

any product you may be promoting, and about which you have to answer questions at presentations and press conferences. Just as we find it difficult to see ourselves objectively, so we find it difficult to see a product whose development we have been close to. We are inclined to overlook some of its advantages, as well as its disadvantages. Seeing it as a stranger might, gives us much greater insight into its true nature.

Step 4

You are now in a much better position to decide what you want to say about yourself. For a recruitment interview you will want specifically to convey the vital point that your experience, training and talent fit precisely into the profile of the job for which you are applying. If you are going to a salary review, you will want to select those achievements (and possibly those faults, too) that show the appraiser that you are worthy of a salary increase or a new company car.

If the purpose of the interview you are anticipating is to present your company or one of your company's products to the media, then you will need to go through the same exercise: determining precisely what you want to say about them. I have found through my consultancy work with companies in the field of Information Technology that even senior executives find it difficult to talk in simple and direct terms to the media – and their problem is not primarily an inability to reduce highly technical information to its simplest form (though that certainly is a problem), it is in knowing exactly what points they wish to convey about their product. As a result, they never give journalists what journalists most need in order to make their interviews worthwhile – a good story. Instead they leave them with a mass of unfocused detail that the journalist has to sort through to find the main points.

The simple advice I give these executives is to think of the product launch or the press conference as an opportunity to tell a good story filled with interesting detail, with anecdote and analogy, that journalists can follow without undue strain and can then convert into a lively and enjoyable feature for their readers. As selling the product is, in the final analysis, the main purpose of the exercise, the better the information, the more lively the feature, and the greater the chance of reaching their target group.

The same may be said about candidates at recruitment interviews and employees on review. If you think of yourself as the product, then you can use the interview not merely to give facts about yourself, but to market yourself. You can do this effectively only if you have clearly in mind the image that you wish to convey. Interviewers need to come away with a clear, distinct impression, to distinguish you from everyone else. Only you can provide them with the means to form this impression, and you can do this only by spending time preparing your lists of achievements and setbacks, and drawing from them a clear and distinct picture of who you are.

Step 5

Having listed your good and bad points, you should now set yourself the task of thinking up the kind of questions you most dread being asked, and coming up with convincing answers. Here is a very small sample of what I have in mind for the recruitment interview:

- What problems do you have in dealing with other people?
- You have been unemployed for . . . (weeks/months/ years). What do you do with your time?
- Why do you think we should give you the job?
- Your record seems to indicate that you've had little experience in . . . How do you think you'd handle this aspect of the job?
- What do you think you could bring to this job that other candidates could not?

- What do you see as your greatest defect?
- Why did you not achieve more in previous jobs?
- Why are you not earning more money at this stage of your career?
- How would you describe the ideal manager?
- How would you describe your last boss?

The list of possible questions is endless.[1] You may have noticed that most of these questions have one thing in common: they relate, not to facts, but to emotions and perceptions. They deal less with what happened than with how the interviewee felt about it. These are the kind of questions that give unprepared interviewees most problems. They also happen to be the questions experienced interviewers prefer to ask, because they help them to find out what you are really like. If the interviewer is properly prepared – and you must always assume they are – they will find out most of the facts they need to know from other sources.

With the media interview, the context in which the interview is conducted will dictate the nature of the questions; but if you are promoting a product or service, it should be an essential part of your preparation to think of all the difficulties and problems that you may have had with its development, and assume that your interviewer will also know about them and will want to quiz you about them.

Armed with this list and your answers to the questions, you will now be in a very good position to meet your interviewer with some measure of equanimity. You should also be able to exert an influence, not only on the content of the interview, but on its overall shape and direction.

Having emphasised the importance of good preparation, I must add a note of warning. Do not flaunt the extent of your preparation. Interviewers do not take to know-it-alls who sit

---

[1]There are a number of books available that give lists of questions most frequently asked in recruitment interviews. See, for example, *Great Answers to Tough Interview Questions*, by Martin John Yate, Kogan Page (1987).

smiling smugly to themselves, enjoying a sense of superiority (often false) and daring the interviewers to catch them out (they usually do!).

DRESSING FOR THE OCCASION

So far we have dealt with the inner you, as it were; the steps to take to focus your mind on the interview; but it is equally important that you prepare yourself physically for your encounter, in other words, your appearance. It is no good going for an interview with facts and figures at your fingertips if you look as though you had spent the night sleeping in the rough.

Some of your preparation, therefore, should be spent deciding how you wish to appear to the interviewer. Do you wish interviewers to see you as super-efficient, as high-powered, as caring more for your resposibilities than your wardrobe, as fashion-conscious or fashion-blind? It would not be appropriate for me to say what you should or should not wear. I am not a clothes consultant and for me to impose my dress sense on you would be invidious. Whether it is right for a man to wear a white shirt or one with stripes, or a woman a suit rather than a skirt, would not be helpful for me to say. So much depends on the circumstances of the interview. For job-hunters, one useful piece of advice I was given by a colleague was to dress, not for the job you have got, but for the one you are going after.

Worrying too much about your appearance is not a good idea. Wear clothes you feel comfortable in rather than those you have never worn before, which may cause you to feel self-conscious and ill-at-ease. On the other hand, wearing old clothes is also not recommended, unless you want to give the impression that you are so involved in your work that you have no time to keep up with fashions. The simple rule to keep in mind is: *dress to convince, not to kill.* In other words, wear the sort of clothes that give the impression that you are at one with yourself and that you know your own worth.

Pay careful attention to any accessories you may want to wear. Heavy jewellery that clanks so loudly that every time you move your hand you drown out your speech is out, and so, too, are those eye-catching ties that eclipse the rest of you so that all the interviewer remembers is the luminous glow hanging from your neck.

Looking good is one thing; you must also make sure that you and your clothes *smell* good. People become very uncomfortable at the mention of personal hygiene, but it is just as important that your hair and nails are clean as that your shoes shine and your tights or stockings are without ladders or holes. Smelling fresh does not mean dowsing yourself in heavy perfume or aftershave, which are every bit as distracting as noisy jewellery.

These seemingly obvious hints are not just about the effect your appearance might have on others, but the effect they have on your own feelings. Simply put, if you look good to others, you feel good about yourself. And that is half the battle won, when confronted by strangers who may or may not be well disposed towards you.

GETTING YOURSELF IN THE RIGHT MOOD

As we shall see when dealing with the subject of rapport, people make up their minds about us in minutes, and because so little time is taken to form these first impressions, our physical appearance plays a vital role. We cannot change what our genes have decreed (except by cosmetic surgery), but we can make the most of what we have got. It all comes down to an inner conviction that we are important to ourselves, because if we do not feel a sense of our own well-being, how are we going to convince others that we are important to them?

For many, what stands in the way of conveying self-respect is fear. We fear, not failing the interviewer, though that is part of it, but failing ourselves — our own expectations. To some this fear can be crippling and can completely ruin the interview. To others even mild anxiety can get in the way of success.

The knack is knowing how to relax. Most of us are not trained to get in touch with our own bodies and to check the amount of stress we may be feeling. If we were, we would be astonished to realise how tense we are much of the time. Even enjoyable activities like conversation can be such an ordeal for some that after a few minutes their muscles tighten and they start to experience mild headaches.

By their very nature interviews are stressful, and if anxiety is one of your problems, it is worth investigating the various relaxation methods available. There are many books and audio tapes on the subject which are designed to aid people to come to terms with their anxieties. Without wishing to sound too pessimistic, none, I think, work completely, except perhaps with many years of practice, because many of our fears are too deep-seated for easy removal; but they certainly can help.

So, too, does simple deep breathing. Tension causes us to breathe from the top of our chests, and this in itself tends to exacerbate the tight breathless feeling we have when we are about to face an interview. Breathing which comes from deep within our diaphragm counters the tension and loosens our muscles, enabling us to relax physically as well as mentally.

What definitely does *not* help is alcohol. Even the most seasoned drinkers, when operating under extreme stress, as when waiting for an interview, cannot gauge accurately how many drinks they need to calm their nerves, and they are likely to drink too much. As even one drink can cause your speech to slur and your reactions to slow down, alcohol seriously impairs your chances of making the right impression. Disguising the smell of drink effectively is more difficult than people realise, and sucking peppermints only gives the game away.

A relaxation method I have used to good effect over the years is what has been called 'visualising'.[2] There is nothing

---

[2]See *Creative Visualization* by Ronald Shone, Thorsons Publishers Limited, 1984.

mystical about this. All you do is take time off to sit quietly and concentrate on the interview you are anticipating. See yourself sitting calmly with the interviewer: hear him or her asking you the questions; see and hear yourself replying to them in a firm and controlled manner. In other words, imagine yourself into the part. Do it a few times before the interview and you will be surprised to see how closely your actual performance resembles the one you visualised.

Some writers compare interviewing to drama, with each participant adopting a particular role. You have heard, no doubt, of even the most experienced actors suffering terrible nerves, to the point of physical illness, before going on stage or in front of the cameras, but because they know their lines, have practised their movements and are thoroughly versed in the character they are playing, they give a tremendous perform-ance. You will do the same if you are properly prepared, no matter how anxious you may feel.

The more you know yourself and act yourself, the better an interviewee you will be. Everything I have said above is to prepare you for that. Experienced interviewers usually see through masks put on by interviewees. Let them see you as you really are: calm and composed, ready to seize the moment and handle with confidence all they throw at you.

CHECKLIST

- Make sure you know where and when the interview is taking place.
- Make sure you know how to get to it. Ask for a map if necessary or get instructions.
- Find out as much as you can about the interviewer or the subject matter of the interview.
- Make a list of your strong and weak points, or those of your product.
- Think up the questions you most dread, and decide on their answers.

27

- Decide what you want to say — what message you want to get across and how you want the interviewer to respond to it.
- Dress appropriately for the part.
- Prepare yourself mentally to give your best performance.
- Avoid alcohol.
- Give yourself plenty of time to reach the interview in comfort.

2

QUESTIONS

'In fact, he is so articulate, so given to lengthy replies to seemingly simple questions and to tangential qualifications of those replies, his hands chopping the air as he goes, that the role of the interviewer is merely to light the blue touch paper and stand well back.' This is how one journalist reported on the film actor, Dustin Hoffman, after interviewing him about a new film.[1]

Is Hoffman the ideal interviewee, or simply a pain? To many interviewers he would certainly be regarded as the latter, while to shy, tongue-tied interviewees struggling to articulate their thoughts coherently, he might be seen as a hero and role model. This chapter will, in an indirect way, attempt to answer that question, or rather, will give you the necessary information to answer it for yourself.

To be accurate, this chapter should be called 'Questions and Answers' because, in interviewing, you cannot have two people facing each other in virtual silence and hope that the 'interview' will somehow succeed, though, a few years ago, when stress interviewing was considered the state of the art, interviewers were required to do just that – sit and stare at interviewees in the (mistaken) belief that it would force them to expose their weaknesses. Thankfully, in its extreme form, stress interviewing is out of fashion, confined, I trust, to the dustbin of history where it belongs. In less extreme forms, however, it is still common, and we shall be dealing with the subject in the chapter on Skills.

---

[1] *The Times*, March 1, 1989.

The process of questions and answers has been compared by one well-known writer on interviewing skills[2] to a rally in tennis where, after the opening serve, each subsequent question is to some extent dependent on the return, i.e. the answer. Ideally the ball should be kept in the air throughout the interview; however, as he adds, the reality often falls short of the ideal. This is either because the interviewer serves a double fault or the interviewee is unable to make an adequate return.

THE PURPOSE OF QUESTIONS

These are used:

- to control interviews
- to obtain information
- to give order to interviews

To control interviews

Interviewers use questions to control the content, the direction, the shape, pace and length of the interview.

Interviewing can be compared to a car journey: the interviewer is the driver and the interviewees are passengers. Questions are like points of reference on the map of the journey which direct both participants towards their destination. Like good drivers who start off knowing where their journey will end, trained interviewers link their questions to the ultimate purpose of the interview; in other words, they first define what they want to achieve from the interview, then they work out what questions they have to ask in order to achieve those results.

The responsibility for formulating the questions belongs to

---

[2]Martin Higham, *The ABC of Interviewing*, Institute of Personnel Management, 1979.

interviewers, not to interviewees, and if, as a result of defective interviewing techniques, interviewers ask wrong or inadequate questions, the fault for that is theirs. Interviewees, however, do have some responsibility to make the interview successful, and they can do this by supplying full and comprehensive answers, no matter how inept the questions are.

It is always safer to assume that interviewers know what questions to ask and how to ask them. However, where interviewers lack experience, well-prepared interviewees should not have much difficulty wresting control of the interview from them by asking most of the questions. With experienced interviewers this is usually very difficult to do. They will, of course, permit interviewees to ask some questions without losing their authority.

To obtain information

It would be correct to say that the better the questions, the better the interview. Perhaps the most common complaint voiced by candidates to recruitment interviews is that the questions were boring. I suspect that in most such cases it is because interviewers see themselves as mere collectors of facts, rather than as interpreters of data. Invariably when that happens, poor decisions are reached and the wrong candidates selected. It would be correct to say that the better the questions, the better the interview.

In media interviews, although good journalists usually arm themselves before a story with all the facts they can get from the cuttings library, sometimes such facts are difficult to discover except from the interviewees themselves. Only the novelist himself would know whether or not a character in his latest novel was based on a member of his family. Interviewers may speculate, and assumptions can be made, but only the interviewee can *know*.

At least, that is what I assumed before one of my journalism students went on an assignment for a magazine to interview an author who had just brought out a new novel. My student happened also to be a great fan of the writer and had read everything he had written, which, as things turned out, was probably a mistake. After she had conducted the interview, she was disappointed in how little information she had managed to obtain, and discussed the problem with me. Looking at her transcript, I soon realised what had gone wrong. Knowing so much about the writer, the interviewer had imposed her ideas on him.

When, for instance, they came to talking about his characters, instead of asking on whom one of them was based, my student posed a leading question: 'X [the character] is your mother, isn't she?' The author puzzled about this for a moment before replying, 'Hmm, perhaps. I hadn't thought of it.' The rest of the interview followed the same pattern, so that by the end all the interviewer had managed to obtain was a series of monosyllabic responses, with which she could do little.

As interviewers can get most facts more cheaply in other ways, those who use interviews solely for that purpose are wasting their time and money.

Interviews go through four stages:

1   Ice-breaking
2   Warming-up
3   The main body of the interview
4   The end

As we have seen, interviews are unnatural contrivances and it is, therefore, to be expected that, no matter how well they relate to each other, the participants will find that communication between them that is based almost exclusively on question and answer is likely to be halting and uncertain, at least in the early stages. Realising this, good interviewers try to put interviewees at ease by finding a subject or subjects of common interest to chat about to put them at ease. The weather, travel and parking problems, are typical ice-breakers. In recruitment interviews, these introductory chats often take place during a short tour of the premises, when interviewers also take the opportunity to talk about the company and its products.

No matter how welcome ice-breakers are to the interviewee, in the hands of unscrupulous interviewers they can be treacherous, and interviewees should remain on guard not to reveal information that they would otherwise prefer to keep to themselves. For instance:

Interviewer: 'Did you find it easy to get here today?'

Interviewee: 'Well, the train was late.'

Interviewer: 'The trains on this service can be very unreliable.'

Interviewee: 'Fortunately I gave myself plenty of time.'

From such a harmless discussion the interviewer may wrongly deduce that the interviewee would have difficulties getting to work on time or in working unsocial hours. Similarly, general enquiries about details of their home and family life may sound to interviewees like conversation, but are, in fact, attempts to evade the laws and codes against discriminatory questions.

In the following example, the interviewee is a woman returning to full-time employment after having a family:

Interviewer: 'Living where you do must be lovely for your children – all that open space to play in.'

Interviewee: 'Yes, we're very lucky.'

Interviewer: 'You're bound to miss all that.'

Whether or not she gets the offer of a job may depend on how she responds to this last remark – and this is before the interview proper has begun.

Here is another example where the interviewer is trying to elicit information from the interviewee that he would not be allowed to enquire about:

Interviewer: 'I expect you had to pack your kids off to school before you set out.'

Interviewee: 'I left that to my husband.'

Interviewer: 'He doesn't mind, then?'

It is not my intention to make you more anxious and suspicious than you otherwise might be, by leaving you with the impression that all interviewers would resort to such subterfuge. The majority of interviewers are honest and fair, or at least try to be, and they will use ice-breakers only to put you at ease. But you have been warned.

To give order to interviews

Interviews, like journeys, should have a destination, known to both participants. Skilled interviewers direct their interviews confidently towards that destination. They work out a list of questions beforehand to help guide them. Unskilled interviewers drive aimlessly, not quite knowing where they are going, asking questions haphazardly and hoping that somehow they will eventually reach their destination.

Questions help to put the interview into context. During the warm-up, experienced interviewers explain what subjects they intend to cover, and in what order. Thereafter, they use questions as sub-headings to tell the interviewee what to expect next.

For example, a journalist interviewing a film director for a magazine profile may say, 'We've talked about your childhood during the war, I wonder to what extent you still revert to it in your films?' This is a signal to the interviewee that the part of the interview devoted to his past is over and the interviewer is now moving on to a new subject.

Interviewees, carried away by their own eloquence, sometimes lose their way, and when this happens, good interviewers remind them where they have been and where they are going by directing a relevant question to them, e.g. 'That has been most interesting, but now I'd like to ask you, when did you decide to start your new company?' Interviewees should be alert to these 'signposts', because they are the interviewer's way of keeping the interview on course.

Some interviewers use questions for the wrong reasons.

They use them to hide both their embarrassment and their ignorance.

I do not have a precise statistic (if one, in fact, exists) but I surmise from my own observation that most executives, if asked, would say they would prefer not to be involved in any interviewing, irrespective of its purpose. Journalists are a different matter, because their work demands that they interview and one of their main reasons for going into the profession is their curiosity to know what makes other people tick. Executives, by and large, do not share this curiosity, even about those they work with. On the contrary, having to ask subordinates questions about themselves causes many of them great discomfort.

For this reason, many executives use questions simply to fill up the time allotted for the interview. Applicants for jobs frequently complain that interviewers ask them questions on subjects that have been clearly stated in their CVs. One recent candidate told me that he was specifically asked in his application form whether or not he smoked; but the interviewer repeated the same question which, in any event, was pointless because, as the candidate later learnt, the company did not have a specific policy about smoking.

The opening question, 'Tell me about yourself,' is another classic time-waster, used primarily by interviewers who are either too lazy or too busy to prepare themselves properly and to think up some clear, useful questions beforehand. It also allows them to calm their nerves and try to develop some focus on the interview while the interviewee is going through their entire life-history. An effective way of handling that question, which will also force the interviewer to concentrate on the shape and development of the interview, is to pause for a moment, think, then ask, 'What specific aspects of my career do you wish to know about?'

Appraising staff is even more difficult for some executives than recruiting, because it involves making and conveying judgements about performance to interviewees with whom they may spend much of their working time. 'I hate telling people how well or badly they have done', is a typical attitude. Preferring to keep the discussion general, appraisers ask vague questions such as, 'How are you getting on?', which is time-wasting. The reply to that one is similar to the previous, 'What aspects of my work are you most interested in hearing about?'

Filling the time with inane questions often hides a lack of preparation. Regrettably, too many interviewers go into interviews hoping that somehow inspiration will come to them and they will find the right questions to ask. Sometimes, of course, they do, particularly if the interviewee is well-prepared and eager to take over; usually, however, the interview starts slowly with irrelevant questions and then grinds inexorably to a confused halt.

A journalist once opened an interview with me about a book I had written by asking, 'What would you say was interesting about you?' He went away with very little, not because I had nothing interesting to say about myself, but because I thought he used the insult to disguise the fact that he had not taken the trouble to do any preparation. I immediately lost all trust in him and all enthusiasm for the interview, and was annoyed that he had wasted my time.

Television, I suspect, is partly to blame for this state of affairs: too many newspaper dramas show reporters going out on a story without preparing anything, yet managing nonetheless to pin the unfortunate victim down with a barrage of brilliant questions. In real life, this seldom occurs; what happens is that the interviewer rummages around in the recesses of his or her mind, desperately seeking questions to put to the interviewee who, quite soon, because of the inanity of the questions, realises what is up and sinks into a morose silence, which only makes matters worse. (In the chapter on skills, I shall explain how to deal with incompetent and unprepared interviewers.)

TYPES OF QUESTIONS

It would not be difficult to write an entire book on questions alone; in fact, to my knowledge at least one has been written.[3] Knowing how to formulate good questions is certainly one of the most important aspects of the interviewer's skill, but it is equally important for interviewees to know about the kinds of questions they are likely to meet, because the more they know, the better able they will be to handle them.

The general rule is: *good questions make good interviews*. A good question is one which:

- encourages interviewees to talk freely, and
- obtains the information required

In addition good questions should be:

- open-ended
- precise
- brief
- relevant
- interesting
- motivating

Open questions usually start with one of the five Ws, namely, Who, What, Where, When, and Why, or How. They require interviewees to answer in full, and make the interview less like an inquisition and more like a conversation. Interviewers who ask open questions show that they are taking the interview and interviewee seriously, because to think them up demands more time and effort than closed questions.

Questions which are too open, however, may be so vague as to leave interviewees floundering, trying to guess what the interviewer is getting at. Shrewd interviewers sometimes ask them for precisely this reason, of course. They are interested to see how the interviewee reacts to them and how they sort out the relevant information from the irrelevant. So, for instance, from the answer to a question such as 'What have you done in

---

[3] *Smart Questions for Successful Managers*, Dorthy Leeds, Sphere Books, 1987.

the last year that you are most proud of?', the recruitment interviewer will be able to assess the candidate's own priorities by the way he or she replies.

In contrast to open questions, closed questions, also called direct questions, tend to pin interviewees down either to a factual reply, or to a monosyllabic 'Yes' or 'No'. This is not always the case, however. Listen, for instance, to BBC Radio 4's justly famous 'Today' morning news programme, and you will hear the presenters, professionals to their fingertips, asking very direct questions of their guests but receiving full and detailed responses. The reason for this is that the programme covers a huge range of subjects so interviews have to be very brief; also most, though by no means all, of their interviewees are experienced in the ways of the media and know not to waste the limited time they have in which to promote themselves or their cause by giving one-word replies.

Precise questions save time because interviewees do not have to work out what it is the interviewer wants from them, and can therefore respond with equal precision. That way the purpose of the interview is fulfilled. Imprecise questions, on the other hand, force interviewees to ask repeatedly for clarification, which slows down the process. Also, not all interviewees have the courage to interrupt and instead answer to what they think is meant. If, as so often is the case, this is incorrect, the interviewer is also thrown off course, so that the entire process comes to a halt, or staggers on unproductively.

Short questions tend to get the interview over with quickly but thoroughly, whereas long questions take up valuable time. Interviewers who persist in asking long questions either love the sound of their own voice so much that they cannot bear to let the interviewee speak, or they have not prepared properly. It can also mean that they are over-anxious and lacking in confidence. They feel that unless someone is talking, filling up the space, as it were, the interview is running out of steam and they have failed to do their job properly. Whichever is the case, long questions are invariably a waste of everyone's time, extending the interview beyond its natural duration. A general rule all interviewers should commit to memory is: *the shorter the question, the longer the answer; the longer the question, the shorter the answer.*

Relevant questions relate, directly or indirectly, to the purpose of the interview. Irrelevant questions go outside the purpose. Some journalists might disagree on this point and say that, like miners, they prefer to let their questions wander over a wide range in the hope that eventually they will strike gold. That may work from their point of view, but it is potentially dangerous for interviewees to be in this situation because, since they cannot see where the interview is leading, they may be drawn into areas they have no wish to enter, and be trapped into giving information they would rather not reveal. If, therefore, you find yourself in this situation, you are perfectly at liberty to ask the interviewer what the relevance of the question is; if you do not receive a satisfactory reply, you should end the interview.

The reason **interesting questions** are good is self-evident: they make the interview interesting. Interviewees want to respond, want to give their best. The opposite situation was described to me by a young colleague who had recently been a candidate for a series of selection interviews:

'They asked all the boring old questions from a list they had in front of them, you know, "How do you view your progress?", "What made you apply for this job?", "Where do you expect to be in five year's time?" I imagine they buy them in a job lot and they think they are not doing their job properly unless they ask them. But you find that if everyone asks them, you tend to answer the first interviewer in full, the second gets an abbreviation of the first and the third an abbreviation of an abbreviation. So you end up doing yourself and the subsequent interviewers a disservice.'

He concluded with a heartfelt sigh, 'Doesn't anyone know any new questions?'

He has, of course, touched upon one of the very great difficulties facing recruitment interviewers: should the interview be a genuine assessment of the candidate's qualities, or merely a means of getting to know the candidate better?

Interviewing as a means of predicting how candidates will function when they are in the job for which they are being interviewed has been the subject of much debate in recent years. Many writers believe that as an accurate predictor of quality, interviews are at best imprecise, at worst, valueless. The problem is twofold. First, interviews are artificial contrivances: a brief meeting of two strangers who communicate through a series of questions and answers. The second relates to the last point: if the questions themselves are faulty, the replies will leave the recruiter with an inaccurate impression of the candidate.

To counter this, interviewers have been trying for years to come up with what they hope will be an infallible list of criteria by which to judge candidates. One of the most frequently used in the United Kingdom is the Rodgers' Seven Point Plan, which assesses candidates on seven main criteria. These are: physical make-up; attainments; general intelligence; specific aptitudes; interests; disposition; and general circumstances. Another is John Munro Fraser's Fivefold Grading Scheme, which categorises candidates by their impact on others, their qualifications, innate abilities, motivation, and adjustment.

Questions are carefully devised, and are repeated in precisely the same way to every candidate, so as to ensure that the interviewer will have a uniform and reliable picture of the suitability of each of the candidates for the job as laid down in the job specification.

That, more or less, is the theory. But this rigidity of questioning leads to the kind of interview my young informant complained of: tedious, repetitive, and uninspiring – just the thing to discourage the bright, ambitious, creative individual that most organisations desperately need. On the other hand, so argue the proponents of the standardisation of selection interviewing, only by comparing like with like, one candidate's abilities with another, in a strict and limited way, is it possible to arrive at a more accurate prediction of how he or she will actually behave in employment.

The debate continues. From the interviewees' point of view,

there may not be a lot in it, because many interviewers use the standard questions, even if they do not use the Seven Point Plan or any of the other assessment methods. This is mainly the result of apathy rather than choice. It is easier to ask the same old questions every time than to think up new, interesting and challenging questions.

Many interviewees actually prefer the conventional questions, because they can work out in advance answers that they hope will convince the interviewer. Books are available with just such answers, and they can be very helpful in focusing the minds of interviewees on the sort of subjects they may be asked about and, more importantly, on the kind of people they are. However, my own view is that the more interesting the questions, the more the candidates will be challenged to think up interesting answers, which gives them the ideal opportunity to present themselves at their best.

I might add that this last point applies, in my view, to all interviews, no matter what the subject. What gives one 'chat show' the edge on another, apart from its host, is the nature of the questions. Those which are designed merely to help the guest promote his or her latest book/movie/record are tedious and predictable; those, on the other hand, that have been well-researched and are imaginatively presented produce the liveliest responses and the best television.

Questions that motivate not only encourage interviewees to give interviewers the information they are seeking, they also give the interview a spirited and energetic forward movement. For both participants, time is money – a point sometimes overlooked by interviewers, who mistakenly believe that interviewees have all the time in the world to spend in their company. Too often they are unprepared and trust to luck or to their innate skills to help them out. Regrettably, the unprepared interviewers are also usually those lacking in innate skills, and the result is time-consuming, directionless conversation. No information of any real significance is conveyed and the purpose of the interview is lost.

As interviewees, you should welcome rather than fear

motivating questions, because they help you to make the most of the brief time you have to present yourselves, your ideas, skills and achievements in the most effective way. They also help you to see the interview as a whole, rather than as a rambling, disjointed series of unconnected questions.

Ideally, interviewers and interviewees should share a common purpose. They should both be focused on the same subjects, on the same areas of discussion, on achieving the same goals. In recruitment interviews, for example, the interviewer is looking for the right applicant to fit the job, and the applicant is looking for the right job to fit his or her requirements. In an appraisal interview both want to reach a joint agreement on, say, future training plans, or to maintain or improve the level of performance for the benefit of their organisation. In media interviews the journalist wants a good story, while the interviewer wants that story to be about them, their product or service.

Whatever the ideal, the reality is that interviews are often battle-fields where personalities and goals clash. The interviewer, for instance, uses the appraisal interview as a means of punishing rather than encouraging the interviewee; the interviewee uses it to voice grievances against fellow employees, rather than as a genuine discussion of his or her own performance to date.

Add to this the very real possibility that the interviewer does not know how to interview. Considering that, apart from professional journalists and specialists working in personnel, not many executives have had any training in interviewing skills, it is not surprising that most do the job amateurishly. There are, of course, executives who, though untrained, have gained experience over the years, but experience alone is not necessarily sufficient to make them competent. 'I don't need training' is their cry; 'After all these years I can do it blind-fold.' Unfortunately, that is exactly what they are, blind-fold by their own prejudices, narrow-mindedness and obstinacy.[4] If this sounds like special pleading for more

---

[4] There is more on incompetent interviewers under the chapter on skills.

training, it is, since I believe that effective interviewing is essential to good management.

There are many questions that do not conform to the ideal open question described above, and, as defective questions tend to be more the rule than the exception, the more you know about them, the better prepared you will be to deal with them. However, subject to certain very important exceptions which we talk about below, it is not for interviewees to challenge interviewers on their interviewing style or to try to correct them. Always assume that interviewers know what they are doing.

Difficult and defective questions to watch out for

- closed
- multiple
- ambiguous
- negative
- hypothetical
- leading
- illegal

The problem with **closed** or **direct questions** is that they are the easiest to ask. In general conversation we tend to ask no other: 'Did you go out on Saturday?' 'Did you enjoy yourself?' 'Did you meet Jane there?' 'Have you been before?', and so on. Open questions starting with the five Ws – What, Where, When, Why, and Who – take more thought, and as most of us are lazy by nature, unless our attention is drawn to their limitations, we go on using them.

If you are faced with an untrained interviewer who is stuck in the groove of the closed question, do what politicians do, use them to launch into the points that you wish to make.

Interviewer: 'Do you think that the economy would be saved by an immediate cut in interest rates?'

Interviewee: 'I'm glad you asked me that. Certainly interest rates are a vital consideration, but more important are our exports, and in my view we are doing all we can to help exporters improve their performance. In the last quarter we have . . .'.

Not all closed questions are wrong. They are used properly by the interviewer:

- to get facts ('How long did you work for that company?')
- to signal a change of direction ('We've dealt with your problems with the new machine. Do you think further training will help?')
- to shut interviewees up if their reply to the previous question has gone on too long ('That's very interesting. Does your service operate internationally?')

Multiple questions are two or more questions strung together. I heard the following multiple direct question in a recent radio interview: 'Do you believe in a federal Russia, and do you think it will work?' The expert's dilemma was whether to answer 'Yes' or 'No' since, it appeared, he was in favour of federation in principle, but thought that, in the particular circumstances, it might not work. In the end, after some hesitation, he ignored both parts of the question and put his point of view about the future of Russia.

This example points directly to the problem with multiple questions. They leave you confused and uncertain as to what the interviewer has in mind, and by replying to one part, you might be giving a distorted version of what you really believe. Rather than attempting to answer and perhaps giving the erroneous impression that you cannot organise your thoughts, ask the interviewer if you could deal with each question separately, or, if you feel confident enough, say, 'Which of these two [or three or more] questions do you wish me to answer first?'

Ambiguous questions are those which appear harmless on the surface but disguise another, less innocent, purpose. In recruitment interviews, interviewers excuse their use by saying that their task is to get behind the mask that interviewees put up. There is undoubted truth in this, and for this reason it is important that interviewees, where necessary, question the point of the question.

What, for example, would you make of this one? 'You must have been to other interviews. How does this one compare?' Is the interviewer looking for compliments, does he want to know who else you have been interviewed by, or is he looking for hints on how to improve his performance? Any or all of these are possible. You could, of course, treat it as an opportunity to be friendly to the interviewer and gain yourself a brownie point or two; but my suggested response would be, 'In what way?' Then it is back to the interviewer to explain himself.

The key for the interviewee is taking an active role, not a passive one. Listen carefully to questions, and pause before replying, to allow yourself time to analyse their meaning(s). If a question is put to you which touches on matters you would rather not discuss, you have to assert yourself by saying so.

Ambiguous questions can be an opportunity to sell yourself. When the interviewer asks you in an appraisal interview, 'How are you settling in?' meaning, 'Are you having any problems with your new colleagues?', you can take the opportunity to show how flexible and responsive you are to new conditions, and that you are a natural team player. When, however, the hidden meaning touches on personal matters that lie outside the boundaries of the interview, then you are within your rights to point this out. But remain calm and good-mannered. It is never a good idea to show open hostility or anger. (See **Illegal questions**, below.)

Negative questions are put either because they reflect the characteristic of some interviewers to look on the pessimistic side of life, or because the interviewers believe that such questions delve deeper and obtain more reliable information.

Here are five typical negative recruitment questions:

- 'We all miss opportunities. What have you missed?'
- 'What are your weaknesses?'

- 'Why is it that you have changed jobs such a lot?'
- 'You stayed in your last job for ten years. Why so long?'
- 'What doubts do you have about your ability to do this job?'

Faced with negative questions, your task as an interviewee is to be positive and to turn the questions around to show yourself in a favourable light. Thus you might reply to the above as follows:

- 'If I have missed anything, I'm not aware of it. I don't look back on my career and think "If only I'd done that." I prefer to look and plan ahead.'
- 'Well, I don't know whether you would describe them as weaknesses, but I tend to be a bit of a perfectionist [or something of a workaholic, or any other desirable management trait], and that can sometimes be a problem.'
- 'Perhaps I have, but every time I've moved it's been to a better one. I am always trying to improve myself.'
- 'My last job was a very good one. They were good employers. I was learning all the time, and loyalty is important to me. But I'd gone as far as I could and it was time to move.'
- 'Like everyone else, I do have doubts, but if I had thought they outweighed my conviction that I could do the job, I'd not have applied.'

No one can argue that negative questions can be useful and should be asked, but the problem arises when the whole tenor of the interview is downward, because ultimately it becomes demoralising. Do not let this happen: fight against it. Remind yourself that no matter how hard they try, interviewers can discourage you only if you let them.

Leading questions are those which suggest the answer expected. Questions such as: 'What were you doing on the night before you stole the safe?' or, 'Where were you standing when you struck the complainant?' would be disallowed in a court of law, because they force witnesses into incriminating themselves.

Like counsel in court, journalists are often too eager to turn interviews into interrogations, and use leading questions to force interviewees to answer as they would like them to:

Journalist: 'What do you think you did to contribute to your company's bankruptcy?'

Company director: 'Well, I don't think I did anything . . .'.

Journalist: 'Presumably, you will now have to consider resigning?'

Company director: 'In the circumstances, I probably will.'

Recruitment interviewers are also guilty of throwing in the occasional leading question: 'Self-motivating people get on in this company. How would you describe yourself?' In this case, it would serve your own interests to give the interviewer the answer he is anticipating: 'I think I can safely say that I am very self-motivating, in fact, I prefer to push myself than have others impose their demands on me.'

But there are circumstances where taking a lead from the interviewer may not help you: 'This job involves a lot of travelling. Do you mind staying away from home for long periods?' Depending on what you want to achieve from the interview, you can either go along with the interviewer and give him the response he wants – 'I like travelling, which is one of the reasons I applied for the job' – or you may have to resist the lead, and answer as befits your situation.

Hypothetical questions ask you to put yourself in imaginary situations described by the interviewer. A typical hypothetical question is, 'How do you see yourself in five years' time?' Replies should always relate directly to the job you are seeking. 'As manager of my department with full responsibilities for customer care, earning in the region of . . .' This shows that you have focused your mind on your vision for a future which is both achievable and desirable.

Questions that start with, 'What would you do if . . .', followed by a hypothetical problem, are asked to find out *how* you would solve the problem – the steps you would take –

rather than the solution itself. They are also sometimes asked to test how you might behave under pressure. Unfortunately, they usually fail to do either. Interviewees are seldom given sufficient information to answer adequately, and even if they answer the question to the interviewer's satisfaction, it is no guarantee that they will act in the same way if the situation did arise. It may prove that they can use their imagination, but this in itself may not be a skill relevant to the job.

Nonetheless, if you are asked a hypothetical question, and if you have sufficient information to answer it, relate your reply as far as possible to your own experience. If you need more details, do not be afraid to ask for them.

Illegal questions – unfair and discriminatory questions – have a long and unsavoury history, and it is a sad reflection on our times that, in spite of statutes and codes which give inter- viewees protection, writers on interviewing should still have to refer to them. The facts are, unfortunately, that they are still being asked. Recently *The Guardian* reported[5] that the Equal Opportunities Commission (EOC) still receives dozens of complaints from women about questions they were asked in selection interviews. The EOC's Code of practice states that if a woman is questioned about her family responsibilities and male candidates were not, then she has a case under the Sex Discrimination Act (1975) for taking them to a tribunal, yet 83 per cent of employers asked women about their family commitments, compared with only 69 per cent for men.

A typical question asked is, 'How will taking this job affect your family?' There are a number of variations, such as: 'What happens if you get married?' or where the woman is already married, 'When do you intend to start a family?' And where the woman already has children, 'Who will look after your children while you're at work?'

To sum up, if you are a woman you should not be asked the following questions:

---

[5] *The Guardian*, October 9, 1990.

- Are you married or single?
- Are you planning to get engaged or married?
- Do you have children? How many? What are their ages?
- What is your husband's job?
- Who do you live with?
- Do you have a boyfriend?
- Do you suffer from period pains or menstrual disorders?
- Are you pregnant or planning a family?
- Do you ever need to take time off during the month?

What do you do if you are asked any of the above, or other questions that might be regarded as discriminatory?

- Establish that the intention behind the question is discriminatory, by asking if the interviewer has put it to male candidates.
- If the reply is that all candidates are being asked the question, you are still not obliged to answer it, and you could counter it by asking what relevance it has either to the job or to your candidature.

Questions relating to race and religion which amount to direct or indirect discrimination are prohibited by the Race Relations Act. If you require any further information on either of the statutes mentioned, guides have been published by the Commission for Racial Equality and the Equal Opportunities Commission.[6]

HOW TO ANSWER QUESTIONS

In addition to the advice given above, here are some general do's and don'ts on answering questions.

---

[6] I draw your attention to the warning made earlier that unscrupulous interviewers may sometimes use the ice-breaking period at the start of the interview to slip in prohibited questions about your personal life.

Do:

- Listen to the questions. Too often, interviewees are in such a hurry to reply, usually out of nervousness, but sometimes out of over-confidence, that they do not bother to hear the interviewer out before responding. Wrong replies mean time is wasted because the interviewer has to start all over again. It can also mean that the interviewee admits information that he or she has not even been asked for.

A television producer of great experience told me that the politicians he least enjoyed working with were those who would never listen properly to the questions, so their answers kept going off the subject, which wasted everyone's time.

The process of replying can be summed up in the mnemonic *LAWDA*:

Listen to the question.
Analyse it to check that you understand what information is being sought from you.
Weigh this against the point or points you wish to make.
Decide on the answer.
Answer.

Do not, however, make the interviewer wait too long while you think up the answer, otherwise the essential forward thrust of the interview is lost and the interviewer may compensate by cutting the interview short, limiting the time you have to put your points effectively.

- Keep your answers brief. Though one cannot make a hard and fast rule, an answer should seldom take longer than a minute; most need not be more than 30 seconds. Long-windedness, the love of one's own voice, is a grievous fault in interviewing, whichever side of the table you sit; so, too, is showing off by parading in front of the interviewer the extent of your expertise, experience or erudition.
- Make your answers interesting and informative. Good interviews, as far as possible, should be a genuine dialogue,

and it is as much your responsibility as the interviewer's to keep the conversational ball in the air by giving replies to questions which go beyond the mere monosyllabic. This does not contradict the previous rule against drawn-out replies. It is not how long you speak, but what you say. If your answers are too brusque and abrupt, the interviewer, to fill up the time, will start asking longer questions, so that the interview becomes one-sided.

● Stick to the point. Answer only the question you have been asked, and ensure that your answer is *relevant*. It is an accepted politician's trick to use every question as an excuse to make political statements, but it is not recommended for ordinary mortals. Nor do I think it works for politicians all the time. The occasional political statement thrown into an interview is acceptable and expected – as is adding a selling point about yourself; but if every question is treated simply as a trigger for a point, relevant or irrelevant, the interviewer loses interest and the interview collapses.

● Keep your message clear by limiting it to one subject at a time. It all comes down to another basic rule, which is: *more is less; less is more*. The more you try to include in your answer, the less the interviewer will get from it; stick to one point at a time and your message will come through loud and clear.

● Keep your answers positive. Earlier we saw how some interviewers emphasise the negative aspect of situations in the belief that it bears a closer relation to the truth. Resist these 'nay-sayers' if you can. You do not have to boast about your achievements, but in a calm manner present your interviewer with a positive, confident image of yourself.

● Take opportunities to pick up on comments made by the interviewer. Being an interviewee does not mean passively waiting for questions and replying to them. Your task is to help keep the conversation going by asking your own questions and taking up some of the slack thrown to you by the interviewer. So, where the interviewer has touched on a point which you think can be elaborated on, take it up and expand on it, even if it is not part of a question. For example, 'I thought what you said in your last question was very interesting, and I'd like to comment on it before we go further.' This shows that not only are you listening carefully to what the interviewer is saying, but you also think he or she is conducting an interesting interview – and few people can resist that sort of flattery. As it also permits you to inject some new information into the proceedings, you win on all counts.

• Ask, if you do not understand a question. It may be one of the defective questions that we have analysed, in which case it is not your fault if you cannot give it a proper reply. Far better to admit this and to request that the interviewer explain what he or she means, than to bluff your way through an answer which could leave you looking evasive, suspicious or plain muddled.

• Use your answers to project something of your personality. In addition to giving information, try to ensure that your replies include something of your feelings as well. Not all your feelings, nor your feelings which are irrelevant to the question, or in excess of the actual situation. But your genuine feelings about the subject in hand. That way you emerge from the interview as something more than a mere interviewee, as a distinct individual in your own right.

Don't:

• Let the interview become an interrogation. This may seem surprising advice to give to interviewees, who, after all, do not control the interview; but as you probably realise by now, my general view is that it is in your power to make the interview what you want it to be. If, therefore, the interviewer fires question after question at you, you can always ask him to slow down so that you can give due thought to each one before responding. Part of how you handle aggressive interviewers is in your physical gestures – I don't mean throwing something at them, though there are occasions when you may be tempted to, but in the self-composed manner you project yourself.

• Regard interviews as examinations you either pass or fail. Think of them more as meetings where, through genuine communication, thoughts and ideas will be exchanged. Idealistic though this may sound to you, it is more fulfilling to consider them in this light than to prepare yourself either for a battle in which there is only one winner, or for a test in which there are only right and wrong replies.

• Use weak, evasive phrases. Wherever possible, answer affirmatively, even if the answer is a negative, for example 'I know' or 'I don't know', rather than 'I'm not sure'. A recent article about the Prime Minister, John Major, commented that his performance in interviews was marred by his persistent use of the phrase 'I think'. In one interview, which lasted under 25 minutes, he used the phrase 43 times! The effect was to make him seem hesitant and diffident. Other phrases to avoid are: 'actually', 'well', 'about' or 'approximately' as in, 'I've been there about five years.'

As a young lawyer, I was advised by my boss never to use the phrases, 'frankly', 'honestly', 'to be honest/frank with you . . .', 'to tell you the truth . . .'. In his view, they invariably revealed dishonesty. That may have been a bit harsh, but I saw his point: if you are responding honestly to a question, you do not have to signpost the fact.

• Lie. Honesty is still the best policy (quite apart from the moral angle). It does not pay to tell untruths for two good reasons: one, you may be found out, with all the embarrassment and inconvenience that may entail including, in certain serious cases, losing your job; and two, even if you get away with it, you have to live with the knowledge that your lie is on record – and that sense of impending discovery may ruin your peace of mind as well as your ability to get on comfortably with your life and work.

When is a lie a lie or a mere exaggeration? It is a lie, for instance, to say that you have obtained certain qualifications when you have not, or to claim that you have worked in a certain organisation when all you did was deliver some papers there when you were a bicycle messenger. On the other hand, on subjective matters, you do not have to give your own deeply felt opinions if by doing so you might jeopardise an offer of a job or cause some other disadvantage to occur. It would not, I think, be regarded as a lie to say that you and your previous boss 'had differences' when, in fact, you loathed the sight of one another. I also think it is acceptable to exaggerate to some extent your contribution to the welfare of your fellow men and women. If, for example, you have been asked what your being part of a team achieved, you are entitled to say, 'I believe that without me we would not have reached our goal in the time it took to do so.' (Don't, however, prefix the word 'believe' with 'honestly', because, if my old boss is right, that will give the lie to your statement.) The opposite approach is to play it down – 'Oh, I'm sure they'd have got on perfectly well without me' – which your interviewer would consider was either false modesty, or proof that you are a twit.

If the question relates to events in your past that you are not proud of, it is acceptable to give plausible reasons and explanations for what happened, so as not to leave the interviewer with a bad impression.

Interviewer: 'In retrospect, do you think you might have done this better?'

Interviewee: 'Up to a point, perhaps, but I still believe that I learnt a great deal from the experience and, as a result, have never repeated it.'

As many countries, including the United Kingdom, have experienced a severe recession and a large number of people have been made redundant, the question arises whether or not to admit to it when applying for a new job. Many opt for 'I took early retirement', or 'I decided I needed a change', but in my view neither of these will do. No dishonour attaches to redundancy, and by accepting the fact, instead of trying to deny it either to oneself or to others, the first step has been taken towards coming to terms with it and seeking new horizons.

● Make jokes, especially against interviewers, the organisation they represent, their products, or third parties who are unable to defend themselves. If you have to laugh at anyone, laugh at yourself, but even that may backfire. Putting yourself down, even humorously, is ill-advised, because you do not have any control over how your remarks are being received by the interviewer. On the other hand, you do not have to treat either the interview or yourself with the kind of deadly earnestness that makes you tense and dull. You can – and should – be serious about the interview, yet still be cheerful and lighthearted. In general, humour is a very difficult and awkward subject. because it is so subjective. A joke to one person is bad taste to another.

● Speak ill of third parties. When recruiters ask you about your previous employers – whether you liked them or not, what their weaknesses were, and so on, they do so not to find out about particular individuals, but to learn more about you and the way you work with others, based on the not unjustifiable belief that your past behaviour is a reliable predictor of the future. The interviewer recognises that your view of your last boss is bound to be subjective – others may not see him or her in the same light – but without casting yourself in the role of villain, or blaming yourself for any disagreements you may have had, you should seek for an answer that is as frank and impartial as possible. For example, you might say, 'Liking or disliking didn't really come into it. She has many qualities for which I admire her, and though we did not always agree, I found working for her stimulating and instructive.' Avoid showing yourself in a good light and everyone else in a bad light, or complaining about others. It is a signal that, unless you get your own way in everything, you are unmanageable.

● Suggest by your answers that the interviewer is stupid or is handling the interview badly. You are, as mentioned before, perfectly entitled to ask, if you do not understand a question, but you should do so in a polite and tactful manner. Interviewers are often as fearful of the interview as interviewees and are therefore more than usually sensitive to slights. It is part of your role to put them at ease and to make them feel they can trust you to answer to the best of your ability. Of course, sometimes interviewers ask really asinine questions. A young graduate I know was asked at the start of the interview, 'Do you lie?' What the interviewer had in mind when asking it was not clear, but while answering in the negative, the candidate was asking himself, 'Is this the sort of man I want to work for?' and deciding long before the end that it wasn't.

● Allow yourself to be bullied into giving answers that reveal information of a personal or confidential nature. Remind yourself before going into the interview that interviewers cannot intimidate you unless you let them. Interviewees in media interviews do not have the protection afforded candidates in recruitment interviews, and journalists pursuing a story may try to make you give personal information about your own life, or that of others. Fortunately we do not live in a police state, so you can resist them, and if they do not recognise that they have gone beyond the limits and are invading your privacy, you can terminate the interview. What these limits are should be discussed, negotiated and agreed upon between you *before* the interview starts.

● Let the interview dry up. Ensure that interviewers have sufficient material from your replies to develop subsequent questions. When you sense that the interviewer is at a loss for something to say, ask a question, or add to an answer previously given. This will not only move the interview towards a conclusion satisfactory to both, but will also help you to get across more information to add to the overall picture of yourself as a confident, dynamic, intelligent individual.

3

RAPPORT

WHAT IS RAPPORT?

When two people meet for the first time, they spend a brief time evaluating each other on what they see and what they hear – in other words, on the verbal and non-verbal signals they receive from one another. Following this, they make the first moves towards establishing mutual trust sufficient to enter into communication with each other with a minimum amount of pauses and interruptions.

This feeling comfortable and being in touch with one another, sharing a sense of common endeavour, of understanding, knowing that the other person values us just as we value them, is what we generally mean by 'rapport', and we know we have achieved it when ideas and thoughts flow easily between us. Equally, we know that rapport has not been established when our communication is marred by hesitancy and suspicion.

In an interview where the parties are strangers, where their status is unequal and where their main means of communication is question and answer, rapport is vital. Without it, the interview will not fully achieve its purpose. Information may be passed, facts obtained and perhaps some feelings revealed, but the whole process has been superficial, leaving both participants with an uneasy sense of incompleteness and failure.

As a journalist I experienced occasions when, despite a full notepad, I felt that I had not really reached the person I was interviewing, but only the façade that he or she had created for my benefit. Similarly, as an interviewee I felt at times that, though I was asked all the right questions and endeavoured to answer them, the interviewer and I had never developed more than the shadow of a relationship. Often this may suffice, because the nature of the interview is itself superficial, but where the subject demands greater intensity of feeling and more depth of understanding, failure to reach rapport is a serious handicap.

Having said that, and considering how difficult it is for two strangers to come together for such a brief period and operate under such rigid though unspoken rules, I still find it remarkable how easily rapport is established; it says a great deal for the flexibility and responsiveness of human beings that, despite all the problems, they can make interviews work.

The degree of rapport required depends on the type and purpose of the interview. In closely structured, fact-finding interviews, such as those carried out in market research surveys, little rapport is necessary, though it should never be entirely absent, since the respondent has to give consent to be interviewed and has also to be sufficiently motivated by the interviewer to want to spend time answering the questions. Realising this, trained market research interviewers endeavour to create a good working relationship with the respondent, knowing that, even within the narrow confines of their task, it can improve the quality of the survey. Equally, a journalist who is reporting an event that took place – say, a fire at the town hall – has to develop a rapport with the witnesses, no matter how superficial, in a very short time in order to get the best story.

At the other extreme, in Freudian analysis, for example, where the analyst attempts to interpret the patient's condition on the basis of dreams and childhood events, hundreds of hours of close working together over a long period is required. Even in less arduous psychotherapy, therapists have to create strong interpersonal relationships with their clients so that they will talk freely about their anxieties and conflicts, and so come some way to understanding the origins and nature of their emotional problems.

HOW IS RAPPORT CREATED?

In most books on interviewing written for interviewers (mine included), heavy emphasis is placed on the interviewer's need to establish rapport, and detailed advice is given as to how they should set about doing it. Failure, we tell interviewers, is serious and usually leads to the collapse of the interview. It has to be admitted that interviewees tend to be treated as though they were passive victims whose physical and mental well-being during the interview is entirely at the mercy of interviewers.

The reality, however, is usually quite different. Interviewees are not helpless victims, pushed into grim offices to sit before fierce tyrants and have their lives and characters destroyed. Nor are they hapless individuals set upon by ravenous journalists intent on drawing from them their innermost secrets. Far from it: interviewees are perfectly capable of holding their own, even where, as in most management interviews, their position relative to the interviewer is subordinate. It follows from this that you share with interviewers the responsibility for forming rapport. Only by both you and the interviewer recognising its importance and both working towards it, can this be achieved.

Rapport involves the ability of both participants to tune into the other person's thoughts – putting ourselves into their shoes, so to speak. The word for this is empathy. When they are interacting with others in normal day-to-day activities, in the office or the pub, most people are able to empathise with others quite naturally and need no training. They listen to complaints from friends and strangers alike; they share in their joys and sorrows in an attentive, unselfish way. However, as soon as they have to face someone in an interview, either as interviewer or interviewee, these normal social instincts fail them, and they confront each other as though they belonged to different species.

Empathy is a quality seldom found in the movers and shakers in our society, those successful executives and achievers who have focused all their energy and determination on the realisation of their own particular vision. They tend to see themselves and those they have to work with as extensions of themselves, rather than as separate individuals. As interviewers and interviewees, therefore, they are unable to put themselves in the other person's shoes because, as far as they are concerned, they not only share the same pair of shoes, they own them!

The line between empathy and sympathy is a fine one. Empathy is understanding how other people feel, sympathy is feeling it and, in addition, waiting to do something about it. Severe though this may sound, there is no place for sympathy in the interview. It gets in the way of the impartiality and objectivity that are essential if both participants are to evaluate each other fairly. Empathy, in the unnatural and contrived circumstances of the interview, has to be worked at. It does not come naturally, nor does it depend on any one factor, but on a whole range of impressions which interviewer and interviewee form in the very few minutes of their meeting each other.

Whether or not an interviewer possesses empathy can be determined by how the room in which the interview takes place is organised. Is it arranged to suit them or the interviewee? Rooms in which the character of the interviewer is too firmly stamped can be very daunting, as interviewees may feel like intruders. Rooms that have as much ambience as a railway station waiting-room, where no care or thought has been given to the comfort of visitors, will not make interviewees feel at ease and eager to give of their best. A vase of fresh flowers, a painting or poster – as long as it is not distracting – can make all the difference. Ideally, the lighting should be bright enough so that interviewer and interviewee can see each other's face clearly, but subdued enough to produce a warm, friendly and relaxed atmosphere. There should be no glare to distract the interviewee, and the provision of hooks on which to put their coats, hats and umbrellas will help considerably to make interviewees feel that they are being treated with dignity.

Since we are addressing the subject of empathy, perhaps this is a good time to look at some of the other responsibilities and problems of interviewers, then see how it is in the interviewee's interests to create the rapport which will lessen these burdens.

THE RESPONSIBILITIES OF INTERVIEWERS

Interviewers have to:

- prepare themselves for the interview by doing the necessary research
- plan how the interview will be conducted, where to start and where to end
- arrange for a suitable time, which can be problematic if, as in the case of selection interviews, a number of candidates have to be seen in one day
- organise a suitable venue for the interview, having in mind that it should be conveniently situated, comfortable and private; and that there should be no disruptions or distractions
- prepare themselves to ask intelligent, interesting, challenging questions that will encourage the interviewees to talk freely and openly
- welcome interviewees and put them at ease
- get the interview started in a brisk and businesslike manner
- ask open questions to encourage interviewees to talk
- control the interview so as not to stray off the subject, while at the same time maintaining a conversational ambience
- listen with complete concentration to everything the interviewees say, keeping their minds clear of all distractions, prejudice, bias and preoccupations

- remain throughout objective, empathetic, patient, no matter what the interviewees do or how they react
- take notes without distracting the interviewees
- keep a vigilant but not obvious eye on the passing of time
- employ the wide range of strategies available, such as probing, summarising, and use of silence, to overcome interviewees' reluctance to cooperate
- cope with interviewees' anger, hostility, tension, fear and other assorted emotional hang-ups
- maintain a steady pace, moving towards the conclusion but at the same time allowing interviewees time to give detailed answers
- end the interview within the time limit, leaving interviewees with their self-esteem intact even if, as in the case of a recruitment interview or performance review, the outcome is bad

A tall order, I think you must agree, so it is not surprising that few but the most experienced and well-trained interviewers are able to carry out all the demands made of them. Appreciating this, interviewees can help interviewers fulfil these demands, provided they know what they are doing.

WHAT INHIBITS GOOD RAPPORT?

The short answer is poor interviewing techniques and ineffectual interviewees. In the chapter on termination, we will be characterising bad interviewers to show how interviewees can deal with them; here we will concentrate on what constitutes ineffectual interviewing from the interviewee's point of view, with suggestions how to improve. I have exaggerated some of the faults in order to make the points clearly.

I have compared an interview to a car journey, or rather a journey from ignorance to knowledge; the interviewer is the driver, the interviewee the passenger. The interviewer/driver

knows the directions, more or less, while the interviewee/
passenger is aware of the route only by the signposts pointed
out from time to time by the driver. Bad driving leads to loss of
direction at best, to accidents at worst, and though passengers
can struggle to maintain some semblance of control by grab-
bing at the steering-wheel, as it were, they have to be very
determined actually to wrest it entirely from the interviewer.

This, however, is not to say that the passenger cannot
contribute either to good driving or to accidents. In fact, they
can play a vital role in ensuring the interview reaches its
destination or, as we shall now see, causing it to end up in a
ditch.

DIFFICULT AND INEFFECTUAL INTERVIEWEES

- brawlers
- defenders
- windbags
- mutes
- mumblers
- fidgets
- racers
- critics
- dawdlers
- smoothies

Brawlers

These are the interviewees who look upon every interview as a
battle they have to win. From the first word to the last, they
fight the interviewer for control, and are a nuisance both to
themselves and to the interviewer who, understandably,
dreads them. They are arrogant and aggressive, believing
themselves to be far more important than the interviewer,

whom they treat with contempt. They persistently interrupt while the interviewer is trying to ask questions; they demand detailed explanations of the meaning of each question, and then argue with that interpretation. They treat questions as a pretext for giving lectures, and are quickly angered if the interviewer tries to interrupt them. 'Would you kindly let me finish' is their response to even the feeblest effort to restrain them.

Perhaps behind their aggressive exterior they are shy and insecure, and are overcompensating by showing that they are afraid of nothing; but unless the interviewer is very skilled and forceful, the effect of their belligerent and disruptive behaviour is to throw the interview into confusion, and ultimately to destroy it.

Defenders

These are the direct opposite of the above. They assume that all interviewers are out to destroy them, and treat every question as a potential weapon meant to strike them down. They develop an impermeable armour to counteract anything interviewers may do to them. The instant they enter the room, they take up their defensive position – arms and legs crossed, hands gripping the chair, lips tight. Their eyes move from the interviewer to the door, ready to make a quick getaway if necessary. Every question is weighed up carefully, but they give away very little in their answers. Sometimes they substitute jokes for replies and try by their wit to distract interviewers from pursuing any line of questioning they feel uncomfortable with – and they feel uncomfortable with most. They also like playing word games, to avoid answering: 'When you say "so-and-so", what do you mean?'

Interviewing them is an uphill struggle and the interviewer, unless very determined, soon gives up, which is what they intended should happen, although why they involved themselves in the interview in the first place, is difficult to fathom.

Prattlers

These are defined in an old dictionary as 'voluble and senseless talkers', which sums them up precisely. They talk ceaselessly, and most of what they say is trivial. Talking is, of course, a natural and necessary part of interviewing; without a full and open exchange between the participants it is dull business indeed, as we shall see when we look at Mutes; but there is talking that leads the interview onwards, and talking that drags it down. Prattlers do not appear to know the difference. A tiny nugget of solid information lodges somewhere in the midst of the thick wad of words that proceeds from them, but mostly the point is lost to the weary listener, unless he or she is very patient and forgiving. If they ever do get to the point, so delighted are they with it that they repeat it again and again. Like Brawlers they tend to make speeches, as well as talk over the questions, but not in an unpleasant or aggressive manner. They are simply unaware of their listener and of the time they are wasting, because they are so wrapped up in their own verbosity.

Mutes

The opposite of Prattlers, Mutes are the bane of the interviewer's life and are even more difficult to deal with than Prattlers. Stopping people from talking is generally easier than trying to make them talk, and because Prattlers reveal a lack of sensitivity to others, determined interviewers feel little reluctance to stamp down hard on them if necessary. Mutes, on the other hand, are often shy and reserved, so interviewers with any sense of fairness treat them with great tolerance and try to help them as much as they can, often to no avail.

Shyness can be a terrible affliction when severe, and those who suffer from it come in various guises and degrees – from the reserved who treat contacts with people, especially strangers, cautiously, to the withdrawn whose shyness borders on the psychotic. Between them are the diffident, who lack confidence in themselves; the timid, who dislike being the object of others' interest; the secretive, who go about in the belief that they have done things that no one else should know about; and the fearful, who are terrified of everyone. Even people who are normally quite assertive can become suddenly shy when sitting in front of an interviewer with a notepad or tape recorder. Finally, there are those who fake shyness in order to obstruct the interview.

Whatever the cause, the effect is that they sit in the interview saying as little as possible, while the interviewer struggles to develop some kind of rapport with them. Not surprisingly, they prefer closed questions so that they need answer only 'Yes' or 'No', and even an encouraging open question will, after a long pause, generate very few words. If the interviewer grows impatient or irritated that only makes matters worse because, at the merest hint of duress, Mutes clam up completely and the interview is *kaput*.

Mumblers

These are a sub-species of the above, who are so wrapped up in their own sense of inadequacy – usually without cause – that they find it difficult to express themselves as they would like. Interviewees who, through no fault of their own, lack a confidence-building educational or social background, exhibit their defensiveness by speaking in low voices and few, poorly chosen words. The more they struggle to articulate their replies, the more tongue-tied they become. Interviewers are forced to struggle to hear what they are saying, and as the interview depends for its success on the free flow of information, those with Mumblers are doomed to fail.

Fidgets

Interviewers can spot them even before they sit down. They enter the room, glancing around suspiciously as though expecting someone to leap out at them from the shadows. They put out a limp hand then quickly withdraw it in case they have done the wrong thing. A nervous smile plays on their lips and they find it difficult meeting the interviewer's eyes. They sit down before being invited to do so, and then commence to wriggle and shift about, continually crossing and uncrossing their legs. Their hands are seldom still: their fingers pluck, pinch or pick at anything within reach – their clothes, the skin of their arms, hands, legs. They also scratch themselves a great deal.

They giggle whether or not the interviewer has made a joke, and they hide their mouths with their hands so that what they are saying is muffled by this defensive barrier. This is a pity because quite often Fidgets have very interesting things to say, but the interviewer has such trouble trying to concentrate, in the face of their constant twitching, that much of it is lost.

Racers

Everything about these interviewees, from their physical gestures to the clipped, brusque manner in which they deal with each question, tells interviewers that they would much rather be somewhere else, doing something far more important. If they do not actually glance at their watches, they give the impression that only their good manners prevent them from doing so. Those whose careers depend on a regular output of manufactured stories about their activities and a steady diet of interviews suffer acutely from this problem. With fame, however, they no longer have the need to court journalists, so they sigh, fidget and look to the heavens to show their impatience, and cut the interviewers off in mid-question to answer them. What they do not realise is that if they allowed the interviewers to do their job, the interviews would finish far more quickly and to everyone's satisfaction.

Critics

'You do not really know what you are doing', and 'I could handle this far better than you' are the messages these interviewees convey, through their irate expressions, fingers tapping ceaselessly on their knees. Sometimes they go further and suggest different ways of asking questions, or even different questions to ask. Perhaps they *could* do better, though one doubts it, but carping about the interviewer's style or method does not improve rapport between them. It only makes the insecure interviewer more self-conscious and less effective, and the confident interviewer more irritable. As a result, time is wasted and the purpose of the interview is not fully realised.

Dawdlers

The impression they give from the tardiness with which they seat themselves is that they have all the time in the world and, given the chance, would like to spend most of it being interviewed. They take an inordinate amount of time thinking about their replies, which they string out into long, tedious monologues. Like Babblers, they treat every question as an excuse for a speech, and rather than sticking to the point they prefer to take complicated detours into subjects that have little to do with the question, or even the interview. This they do in slow, measured speech with little change in tone or rhythm, and if interviewers manage to stay awake, they will find they have gained little for their trouble.

Smoothies

Their grins wide, their eyes bright, their voices loud, their handshake firm to the point of painful, they breeze into the interview as though the interviewer was their nearest and dearest friend. Worried, anxious? Not them. Why should they be? They love being interviewed and they love the interviewer, even though they only set eyes on him or her five minutes ago. They are determined to make this a pleasant time for everyone, so they give the answers they think the interviewer would like to hear, whether or not they reflect their true feelings. They laugh at all the interviewer's jokes and nod their heads vigorously to show that they agree with everything the interviewer says. Ingratiate, ingratiate, is their aim, in the belief that it will get them what they want out of the interview. Sometimes, with inexperienced interviewers, it does; but experts see through them at once and discount most of what they tell them, so all that effort goes to waste.

It is a pity, because Smoothies have a good idea of what being an interviewee is about; the only trouble is that, lacking sincerity, they caricature the role and spoil it for themselves.

As I said above, I have deliberately exaggerated these flaws to make the point that, though interviewers have the main responsibility for achieving rapport, if they do not succeed, the blame may lie with the interviewee. I also wanted to show that these shortcomings all have one factor in common: the interviewee's lack of empathy. They are so wrapped up in themselves that they are incapable of putting themselves in the place of the interviewer, or of realising the detrimental effect they are having on the interview itself.

Empathy is essential to good rapport – on both the interviewer's and the interviewee's part – because each has to be able to look into the mind of the other, to be in touch with the other's feelings and reactions, in order to assess their own behaviour and adjust it according to how they are being received. The characters portrayed above all share the same chronic inability to do this.

I do not want to give the impression that ineffectual interviewees alone are to blame for interviewing disasters. We will see in a later chapter how poor interviewing styles can prevent the most responsive interviewees from giving their best performance. Nor do I wish to suggest that most interviewees fall into one or another of these categories. This is very far from the truth. None of us is perfect; we all on occasions exhibit some of these characteristics; but most of us go into an interview with the very strong wish to put on our best show. Interviewers know this and, if they are any good, will share this desire; thus, between the two, a workable relationship will inevitably follow. Skilful interviewers ought, moreover, to be able to establish a rapport with all but the very worst interviewees.

HOW TO MAKE RAPPORT WORK FOR YOU

Maintain your poise

Interviews belong to the interviewees, or should do. Their purpose is not to make interviewers feel better about themselves by giving them thirty minutes or more to demonstrate how powerful and dominating they are, or alternatively, how nice they can be to lesser mortals, but for them to obtain information upon which they can act for the ultimate betterment of all. If interviewers take the effort to establish good rapport with their interviewees from the start, they should achieve this purpose in an efficient and businesslike manner.

The central theme of this book is that interviewees should approach interviews as active participants, and that the best interviews are those where both participants are fully engaged.

Having said that, it would be wrong of me to suggest that you can always run the show. In fact, you are in something of a dilemma because the more active you are, the greater the damage you may be doing to rapport as well as to the impression you are making on the interviewer. In recruitment interviewing, this can be a serious problem. You do not want to leave the interviewer thinking that you are bossy, arrogant, or difficult to get on with; nor do you want to appear as someone so submissive that you will do whatever you are asked. How to resolve that dilemma is something we shall attempt to tackle in the rest of the chapter.

Rapport is established even before you and the interviewer meet. Good interviewers, knowing the anxieties many interviewees experience, try to create an environment in which you can relax. A pleasant waiting room with magazines and newspapers to read, perhaps with a cup of tea or coffee provided, goes a long way towards achieving this. Increasingly, in recruitment interviewing, candidates are taken on a short tour of the company's premises to show them something of its activities. In addition to putting candidates at ease, this also allows them to be told a little about the company.

Unfortunately, some interviewers neglect this vital stage of the process and you may find yourself left to your own devices in a cold, empty room with nothing to do but worry about what is about to happen next. Interviewers from the 'stress-is-good-for-you' school actually believe that putting interviewees in uncongenial surroundings tests their strength of character and purpose, and forces them to perform at their best. Happily, these interviewers are in a minority.

It is more likely that interviewers do not have sufficient wit or empathy to realise that allowing interviewees to languish on their own for an unnecessarily long time in uncomfortable surroundings demoralises them and, as a result, they have to make a more determined effort to establish rapport with them.

Whether interviewers behave in this manner deliberately or (giving them the benefit of the doubt) because they have no empathy, this is a crucial test for you. If, therefore, you find yourself sitting in an empty waiting room with only your rapidly beating heart for company, or in the interviewer's office, staring at the wall above his head while he makes arrangements for the squash game that evening, you have to endeavour to maintain your poise. Do not let them break your spirit, but remember that, whatever happens, you have gone into the interview to make the most of it and you will not be deflected from achieving this. Remember also: *the interviewer cannot intimidate you unless you allow it.*

You may also meet interviewers who, if anything, are even more nervous than you. You will recognise them by their inability to meet your eye, their soft, uncertain handshake, their murmured greeting. Do not be tempted into thinking that the interview will be a walk-over. On the contrary, because nervous interviewers tend to let matters take their own course, which means, in effect, that you will be in the driver's seat, you will have to chart the route, and you will have to know when to come to the end. Since you are also trying not to give them the impression that you are trying to dominate them, you will have your work cut out maintaining your poise and achieving your purpose.

Most interviewers are reasonably confident, fair-minded people who will want you to see them at their best – as polite, friendly, businesslike and purposeful – which is precisely how you will want them to see you.

Make a good first impression

The opening minutes of the interview are crucial, because it is during this brief period that you and the interviewer receive your first impression of each other. First impressions and rapport are dependent on each other. Interviewers and interviewees should feel comfortable with, and positive towards, each other in order that a relationship of trust is developed between them. The better the first impression, the better the rapport; and vice versa.

A few points, then, about first impressions:

- Four minutes after meeting is all it takes for people to make up their minds about each other.
- Having made up their minds, they tend not to change them.

- Rather than altering their initial reactions, people prefer to find evidence that will confirm them.
- First impressions linger on, and it takes both time and effort to make people change them.
- First impressions are mainly based not on reasoned evaluation, but on irrational factors such as appearance, demeanour, expression and posture. In other words, it's not what you *say*, but what you *do*.
- The 'halo factor' plays a vital part in formulating first impressions. (See below.)
- First impressions are more likely to be favourable if the parties share a common background and culture, as well as an assumption as to what the interview is about and how it is to be conducted.

The 'halo factor'

The 'halo factor' is a very common human weakness, one that most of us at some time in our lives have been guilty of. How many can claim never to have responded positively to a stranger on first meeting simply because of a shared interest, only to find on closer acquaintance that there is nothing else about them we like?

It is, however, of vital importance in recruitment interviewing. What happens is that on the basis of one attribute – often a relatively insignificant one – the interviewer assesses the candidate favourably, whether or not the candidate fits the requirements of the job. The interviewer may, for instance, have seen on the candidate's application form that she is keen on amateur dramatics, an interest the interviewer shares. Even before they meet, the interviewer is well disposed towards her, and will view all other aspects of the candidate in the same approving light, exaggerating her strengths and overlooking her failings.

Not only is this an unreliable way to select someone, it is also unfair to other candidates who may be better qualified but do not indulge in play acting. It is, moreover, potentially costly to the organisation, because the lucky candidate may turn out to be completely wrong for the job.

The 'halo factor' can also work in reverse. Here the interviewer rejects the candidate out of hand, because of one small detail. When I was a young lawyer my boss had a strict rule which was never to trust a man wearing a bow-tie. A rigidly honest man, he would no more employ a bow-tied solicitor than use his clients' money for his own purposes. But it meant that he might easily have overlooked a suitable but, in his view, improperly dressed applicant in favour of one who was in every other respect unsuitable.

This point was aptly illustrated in a cartoon showing an interviewing panel of four men who were interviewing a fifth man. The men, including the candidate, were carbon copies of each other in both dress – dark business suits – and appearance – thick wavy, black hair and bristling moustaches of the type favoured by airline pilots. The caption read: 'We have to say, Smith, we really like the look of you.'

The cartoon points up the potential absurdity of the 'halo factor', that, irrespective of their qualifications, recruiters tend to choose candidates like themselves.

Project your 'persona'

The Latin word *persona* means mask, and psychologists use it to denote that part of our personality we usually show to others, keeping our true thoughts and feelings to ourselves. We do not use the same persona when we are with our colleagues at work as when we are with our parents or our children, our close friends or spouses. Obviously many of our characteristics remain the same, but certain important ones change, so if someone close to us were to see us in surroundings they have never seen us in before, they would quickly notice the difference.

This notion has vital consequences for interviewing, especially for those first few minutes when rapport is set up. The mask or face you present to the interviewer is something you can control. This does not make it a false you, a disguise in the sense that it hides the real you, but one of the many facets of your total persona.

Unless we are very self-assured or very thick-skinned, most of us are apprehensive before an interview. It is right we should be. We are, after all, entering unknown territory, depending on a stranger to guide us along. Some of us of an even more nervous temperament suffer awful pangs of fear and, in the worst cases, are physically sick.

The point to remember is that the face that you present to the interviewer need not be the 'true' you, with all your fears, anxieties, self-doubts and uncertainties. It can be, if you choose, the other you, the one who is eager to make a good impression and to establish a genuine relationship with the interviewer. Nothing obliges you to present the fearful, anxious face to the interviewer. If you have taken all the necessary steps to ensure that you are properly prepared for the interview, you can choose to present a more confident and self-assured persona, because we all have it in us to do so.

That said, it is, of course, both undesirable and impossible that you should try to be a different person to everyone who interviews you – a man or woman for all seasons. You cannot and should not try to change your personality merely to suit the prejudices of the interviewer. You cannot know in advance what expectations the interviewer has of you, and even if you pretend to be what you are not, any experienced interviewer would probably spot the dissimulation within a very short time.

Interviews do not last for ever. At the most, they will take up about an hour of your time and, no matter how fierce the interviewer is, he or she cannot cause any physical harm to come to you. True, they can deny you the job you have applied for; they can appraise you negatively; they can also, if they are playing some kind of power game, endeavour to make you feel small and inadequate. But they cannot break you *unless you let them*. Whatever happens, you will live to interview another day.

Be what you want to be

Some years ago an American psychologist, Dr Eric Berne, developed a theory of personality which he called Trans-actional Analysis (TA). In two famous books, *Games People Play* and *What Do You Say After You Say Hello?*, he put forward the proposition that the human personality is divided into what he called the 'ego states' which we all assume in our relations with others. These are the 'games' and 'roles' we all play.

In the relationship between interviewers and interviewees, TA posits that interviewees may adopt one of the three roles: the Parent, the Adult, or the Child. As Parent, interviewees will probably be older, more set in their ways, critical of inter-viewers in general and inclined to teach them how to do their job. They will make little effort to establish rapport unless they are of the same age and background as the interviewers, in which case they will be able to join forces in criticising others: the youth of today, modern values, and so on. This can be a major advantage to the Parent interviewee.

Interviewees who assume the state of the Child are, in the main, anxious and lacking in confidence, worried about their careers and where they are going in life. They look upon the interviewers as Parent, depending on them to set the pace and ask all the questions. They tend to take a submissive role, rather than making a positive contribution to the outcome. Child interviewees respond willingly to questions, but their answers are tailored to please the interviewer and are not true reflections of their feelings. Rapport is illusory, because the interviewers are seeing interviewees in their most dependent, least mature state. Submissive Child interviewees also tend to bring out the worst of the Parent in interviewers, encouraging them to abuse their authority.

The Child ego state, which most of us move in and out of at various points in our adult lives, also incorporates some of the qualities that make us interesting and stimulating to be with: gratitude, playfulness, inventiveness and imagination.

Therefore, though many of us assume this state when being interviewed, we are not doomed to a passive, helpless role, but are capable of asserting ourselves sufficiently to form an effective and responsive relationship with our interviewers.

The most mature of the three ego states that Dr Berne proposes is the Adult, who is calm, composed, logical, organised, objective, unemotional, and able to handle all manner of stress without any difficulty – precisely what we all aspire to as interviewees, but seldom achieve. The fact that we do not should not deflect us from making the effort, without losing sight of the fact that the Child in us also has a place, and so, too, has the Parent, since most of us are made up of all three attributes. The importance is to balance them and to know when any one of the three is inappropriate. Thus, for instance, when we feel that we are becoming submissive, falling into a dependency so that our personality is becoming swamped by that of the interviewer, then it is time to summon up the Adult in us and bring into the relationship a degree of equality.

It must also not be forgotten that these ego states apply equally well to interviewers. They, too, can be Child – helpless, dependent, unreliable, but also playful and friendly; Parent – firm, authoritative, bossy, biased; or Adult – patient, fair, logical.

Ideally, rapport is best achieved when both participants are in the Adult ego state, acting in a mature, unemotional way, questioning, listening and arriving at an outcome satisfactory to both, with perhaps some of the wit and playfulness that characterises the Child state. But in real life, this seldom happens. More often than not the Child submits to the Parent, or two Parent ego states battle for supremacy.

You are what you want to be and if, like most of human kind, you are a mixture of all three ego states, you can choose which one would be most appropriate for the interviewer. If, for instance, you are about to be interviewed about the romantic bestseller you have just written, you will probably not want to appear as the pushy Parent or the logical, dispassionate Adult, whereas the defenceless Child may be just what the journalist is looking for.

Reassure the interviewer

It may seem odd to suggest that interviewers need reassuring, but, the fact is, many find interviewing even more arduous and taxing than interviewees. In order to establish rapport with them it is necessary that you make them feel they can trust you, just as much as you need them to reassure you that they can be trusted.

Some senior executives, in spite of their exalted positions, suffer from fears and uncertainties, and do not enjoy being exposed to the critical gaze of sceptical and suspicious interviewees. Lower down the management scale, many are quite timid people, who panic when things go wrong – they are interrupted by an urgent call, the interviewee shouts at them, or, much worse, starts to cry. Many, too many, think they can go into the interview unprepared, only to find that they lose their way and dry up within the first five minutes. Then there are those who have not worked out clearly in their minds what the interview is about – whether it is, for example, to appraise, discipline, or counsel the interviewee – and do not know what questions to ask.

Why, you might ask, is it your responsibility to help them? What do you get out of it? The answer is good rapport, which, in turn, means substituting real communication for a mere exchange of half-digested facts and ideas. Only when that is achieved, can you be assured that you have got the most out of the interview.

How, then, do you reassure the interviewer?

Contrary to what some interviewees believe, interviewers are human, and like all human beings, want to be loved, or at least to win the approval of others. What they need from you is confirmation that they are conducting the interview effectively. By conveying this message to them you are rewarding then –

and, as Michael Argyle wrote some years ago, 'Rewarding-ness' is the key to 'effective social influence: if A is sufficiently rewarding to B, *he has more influence over B*, [my italics] because there is the possibility that the rewards may be withdrawn.'[1]

As an interviewee in a subordinate position, you cannot tell interviewers how well they are doing. You cannot say, for example. 'I know I am being difficult, but I think you are doing a magnificent job getting any useful information out of me.' You have to *show* them through your gestures and your facial expressions.

These days politicians, public speakers, indeed, all who have something to sell through the media, are trained in the rudiments of non-verbal communication. The esoteric secrets of body language have become the bedrock of courses on interpersonal skills. Yet there are still people who view the subject with scepticism. They do not deny that it exists – we all know from observation how much we can tell what others are thinking by how they are acting – but they claim that its importance has been exaggerated.

In my own seminars I still occasionally get critical reactions when I suggest that the arms-folded, legs-crossed posture indicates defensiveness. 'But I always sit like that, I find it more comfortable', the trainee insists with genuine puzzlement.

The misunderstanding that exists with the interpretation of body language is in making a direct connection between a single gesture and a state of mind. Sitting with legs crossed does not necessarily mean that you feel the need to defend yourself. Similarly, when you scratch your nose it may be itchy and is not a sign of doubt or suspicion. It is only when the gesture or the posture is 'read' together with other gestures that an observer can make a fairly safe assumption about the 'message' being conveyed.

'Reading' body language is like reading any written text: the meaning does not come from single words, but from groups of

---

[1] Michael Argyle: *The Psychology of Interpersonal Behaviour*, Penguin Books (1972).

words collected together in sentences. Similarly, to understand body talk accurately is not to see the gesture in isolation, but linked together with other gestures and expressions to make up a 'statement' of mental disposition.

Therefore, if an interviewee rubs or touches her nose and, at the same time, clears her throat and looks down at her shoes, the combination of gestures indicates some doubt or uncertainty about the truthfulness of her reply.

The other important point to remember about body language is the consistency or inconsistency between the verbal and non-verbal communication (better known as 'congruence' and 'incongruence'). Simply put, this means that if a person says one thing but their body says another, they may be hiding something, or they may be unsure of themselves, or be saying one thing while believing another. They may also be lying. People trained to understand body talk will recognise the inconsistency, and will make a point of probing deeper for the truth.

Hamlet's observation, 'That one may smile, and smile, and be a villain' is a much-quoted example of incongruence. Mafia hit-men, if Hollywood is to be believed, approach their intended victim with gestures of warm friendship – handshakes, kisses on the cheeks, and much shoulder slapping – only to whip out their pistols and shoot him dead.

Rewarding body language

It is through the following gestures and expressions that you reward interviewers, reassuring them that they are conducting a good interview. By doing so, you will put them in your debt, which should go a long way towards helping you achieve what you want from the interview.

- sit comfortably in an upright but relaxed posture, feet together, legs uncrossed
- rest your hands on the arms of the chair or comfortably in your lap

- look at your interviewers with an interested expression, particularly when they ask you questions
- keep your head raised when you listen and when you speak
- lean forward when the interviewer asks you a question
- nod your head intelligently whenever the interviewer tells you something
- stroke your chin occasionally to show that you are concentrating

For the reasons given, avoid the following gestures:

- fidgeting, scratching, biting your nails, which all signal unease in the interviewer's presence
- covering your mouth with your hand when replying and muttering, which also signal nervousness and lack of confidence in the interviewer's abilities
- crossing both arms and legs, clasping the chair or your upper arms, or balling your hands into fists, which show you are feeling threatened by the interviewer
- leaning backwards, looking away from the interviewer and crossing your arms, which convey the message that you do not approve of the interviewer
- gazing fixedly at some point in the room, other than the interviewer, or looking down to examine your hands or the carpet, which are sure signs of a lack of interest in what is going on
- pointing your body towards the door, which could be signalling your desire to get out of the interviewer's office
- kicking your foot or tapping your fingers, which tell the interviewer that you are impatient, either to speak or to leave
- propping up your head with the palm of your hand, yawning, staring blankly at the interviewer, or scribbling on some paper, which shout louder than words that you are bored, bored, bored!

There are, of course, many other combinations of gestures that will either delight or demoralise the interviewer and you are aware of all of them subconsciously, if not consciously. However, a word of caution: to become too aware of them will make you appear unnatural. 'To thine own self be true, And it must follow, as the night the day, Thou canst not then be false to any man', was Polonius's advice to Hamlet. Do not pretend to be what you are not, because you will not succeed in convincing the interviewer. Rather aim to be the aware, interested, involved interviewee that you really are, with every inch of your mind and body, and you are bound to succeed.

CHECKLIST

- See yourself as you would like to be seen by the interviewer and, from the demeanour you adopt, expect to be treated with respect and dignity.
- Do not take yourself too seriously, otherwise you will become pompous, self-opinionated and boring.
- Your appearance is important, but even more important is what you are feeling inside. If you are in control of your emotions and have your sights fixed firmly on achieving your purpose, you will convey this to others.
- Plan more, worry less. The better prepared you are, the more confident you will feel and the more time and energy you can devote to building a relationship of trust with the interviewer.
- Do not be overwhelmed, either by the interview or by the interviewer. Remember that, no matter how long it lasts, the interview must end and you are free to go.
- Concentrate your attention on what is happening at the time and put out of your mind the consequences of the interview which, in any event, you cannot foresee.
- Focus on the interviewer and the questions you are being asked, and do not worry about the effect you may be having on them.

- At the start of the proceedings take your cue from the interviewers. If they want to get on with the interview without preliminaries, let them do so. On the other hand, if they want to engage in small talk, join them by engaging in conversation. Hearing the sound of your own voice will help to put you at ease and give you confidence.

- Stay off politics, religion and personal remarks about the interviewer's company, organisation, product or service. Even an apparently innocent comment may cause offence. Jokes are always dangerous, because they depend for their effect on both the narrator and the listener sharing certain common assumptions about life, which you may not do. Sport is a safe subject, but only if you are genuinely interested and, more to the point, they are, too.

- Be aware of interviewers who surreptitiously try to obtain information through innocuous questions about your personal circumstances.

- Do not get so involved in the warm-up that you take up valuable time. Some interviewers have the mistaken idea that only their time is important. Convince them that this is not the case by showing yourself to be businesslike and purposeful. You and the interviewers are not going to be friends for life; only friendly acquaintances for the half-an-hour or so that you are together.

- Take the initiative if it is being offered. Volunteer information when you can; the interviewer may thank you for it.

- Do not let the interviewer's inattention put you off. They may have been interviewing all day and are probably tired. Nonetheless, you are entitled to have your say, even if they have heard it all before. Say it: but keep it brief and to the point. Remember the rule: *boredom (yours or the interviewer's) kills rapport.*

4
SKILLS

QUALITIES OF SUCCESSFUL INTERVIEWEES

The three main qualities which distinguish effective interviewees are:

- enthusiasm
- confidence
- lucidity

Enthusiasm

Enthusiasm is a wonderful quality, not only in interviews, but in every undertaking in life. It does not always win first prize, but it carries one through many a setback. It is difficult to describe in so many words, but it is a combination of energy and determination, with just a dash of tension to give the edge to speech, posture and expression.

Enthusiastic people are those who enjoy what they are doing and are able to convey this sense of enjoyment to those they are with. They are free from self-consciousness and are more in control of their circumstances, because they are not so concerned by the effect they are having on other people as on what those people are saying or doing.

Enthusiastic people are what one writer calls 'life

affirmers'.[1] They are emotionally stable and are not easily upset. They decide on a course of action after examining the pros and cons, then carry it through. They are confident, with a strong sense of their own self-worth, but they are not arrogant or complacent; nor do they believe that they have reached their full potential.

Life to them is not a series of accidents, but has some order to it, and accordingly, once they have a goal in mind, they do not merely leave matters to chance or to take their own course, they plan and prepare themselves for it. They are optimists, but they also have a strong sense of reality, and are flexible enough to cope with changes.

When describing life affirmers, the writer could have been describing the ideal interviewee. Regrettably, most of us fall quite a long way short of the ideal, and for those who have spent many months searching for a job, enthusiasm is a quality that becomes harder and harder to summon up at will. But we can, with effort, all aspire towards it. How enthusiasm is conveyed to interviewers will be considered below when we discuss body language.

Enthusiasm can be overdone. In the old meaning of the word, 'enthusiasts' were people who deluded themselves into thinking they were possessed by divine spirits. Though this is not likely to be your problem, it is nevertheless important that you guard against over-enthusiasm. You want to show interviewers that you are pleased to be in their company and that you are involved in the interview, but you want to avoid overwhelming them with your fervour.

Your step should be light, but you do not have to run into the room. Smile, but do not grin. Keep your eyes on the interviewers, but do not stare at them with a fixed gaze. Wait for them to make the first move before you shake their hand and do not crush their fingers or dislocate their shoulder in your enthusiasm. Do not waste their time or yours with incessant chatter before the interview starts. Be particularly careful

---

[1] Clive Wood, *Say Yes to Life*, J. M. Dent & Sons Ltd (1990).

not to be carried away by camaraderie and make references to their appearance or clothes, because you risk seriously embarrassing, or even insulting them. When you enthuse about their clothes, furniture or paintings, they may mistake your intentions and think you are poking fun at their taste.

Confidence

The great menace to peace of mind is fear of failure. It is that more than anything else that shatters our confidence and makes cowards of us all. In extreme cases it prevents us from undertaking any new enterprises, with the result that we stay in jobs we detest, and live in surroundings and with people we dislike.

In America I picked up some good advice from, of all things, a sachet of sugar which had the following wise words printed on it: 'If you have tried to do something and failed, you are vastly better off than if you had tried to do nothing and succeeded.'

Even if we fail at the interview and do not get the job or the rise we wanted, or the magazine that interviewed us decides not to use our interview, at least we made the effort and we have to believe, because it is true, that there will be other interviews, other chances to prove ourselves.

Going for a new job, confronting your boss to ask for a rise, or agreeing to be interviewed by a newspaper is taking a positive step towards achieving a goal. The fact that you have done so means that you have conviction in your own abilities. Then, instead of wasting your time worrying whether or not the interview will go in your favour, spend your time making the necessary preparations. (See the chapter on preparation.) After that, leave the rest to chance because, like it or not, chance also plays its part.

Lucidity

This, the third most important quality shared by effective interviewees, means clearness in reasoning and expression. I prefer the word to 'clarity' because it implies brightness, not only in intellect, but also in mood and tone.

Your aim as an interviewee is to reply to questions in an interesting and intelligible way, so that interviewers are not left confused or uncertain as to what you mean. Never underestimate them, but at the same time do not assume they know more about the subject than you.

Most businesses and professions have developed their own 'language' in which the members talk freely to each other. Problems arise when they have to talk to people who do not share their language. Interviewees working in high technology, for example, spend most of their time either talking to computers or to each other, and they therefore find it difficult to communicate with those who have not had their background or training. Some of the information they have to convey is, admittedly, very abstruse, but much of it can be reduced to simple terms without it losing its meaning.

Lucidity means caring about being understood, taking the time to translate the language of your profession into one that interviewers can understand. It comes back to empathy. Ask yourself whether or not you would understand what you were saying if you were the interviewer, and if the honest reply is 'No', adapt your response accordingly. Placing interviewers in the awkward position of having to admit their ignorance is not going to make them respond positively to you.

Preparation helps, but beware of over-preparation. At its best, interviewing is a creative process that leaves you both changed for the better. If, however, you are so well prepared that nothing is left to chance, you will destroy the element of spontaneity that makes it an enjoyable and stimulating experience for both of you.

OVERCOMING NERVES

Experience teaches that the things we most fear seldom come to pass, and when we think back we wonder what it was we were so worried about. Interviews are important, and it is necessary that you take them seriously, but go about them in a practical manner. The more emotion you put into them, the less efficient you are going to be.

Confidence is catching. Contrast sitting in a car with a driver who knows what to do and moves off smoothly into the flow of traffic, with someone who grinds the gears to jerk the car into motion, then stops with a juddering halt at the first intersection after barely missing an approaching vehicle. In the first, you can relax because you know that the driver has everything under control. In the second you are constantly on tenterhooks in anticipation of an accident.

The same applies to interviews. Good interviewers react positively towards confident interviewees because they know that, between them, they are going to reach their destination, i.e. they are going to achieve the purpose of the interview, without accidents. With confidence comes control, and with control comes the power to take the initiative.

Taking the initiative

Interviewees who are in a subordinate position to the interviewer have to face a difficult problem, one that does not arise where the positions of the participants are equal, as in most media interviews. The problem is how to assert themselves and take the initiative without challenging the status of the interviewer.

The line between assertiveness and discourtesy can be very thin, and interviewees who are determined to make their mark can easily overstep it, angering the interviewer and in so doing losing, not merely the initiative, but the chance to promote themselves. Yet, at the same time, passive interviewees who make no impression on interviewers achieve nothing.

Research in recruitment interviewing tends to show that, the less interviewees talk and the more submissive they are, the better their chances are of being acceptable to the interviewers.

Nicely behaved, conventionally dressed candidates are preferred to those who are, in the estimation of interviewers 'over-dominant'.[2] The situation is complicated by the fact that, though interviewees are expected to behave submissively during the interview, they may have to act in exactly the opposite way in their jobs. A meek, unassertive salesperson, for example, who never tried to push through a deal, would not keep the job for long.

Striking a balance between being passive and being positive, knowing when to show independence of spirit and when to be pliant, is a matter of subtlety and discretion in which both tactfulness and empathy play an equal part. At no time, however, no matter how assertive you are, should you ever display bad manners and rudeness to interviewers.

We saw earlier how important first impressions are. People make up their minds about each other in about four minutes, and these first impressions remain to the end. This is particularly the case in unstructured interviews, which depend more for their success on the rapport established between interviewer and interviewee, than the structured interview in which the interviewee is processed through a rigid set of questions. Interviewees who enter an interviewer's office with a sense of their abilities and a consciousness of their worth are much more likely to make a positive impression that those who slink in, eyes cast down, as though apologising for their intrusion on the interviewer's valuable time.

Even though you may not be entirely convinced that you are the best candidate or the most important guest on the interviewer's chat-show, you should make every effort to appear as though you are, because, as we also saw, interviewers rely far more on appearance, manner and expression to form their impressions than on what interviewees tell them.

Being nervous before interviews is perfectly natural, and the best interviewees usually are. Only those with little

---

[2] Michael Argyle, *The Psychology of Interpersonal Behaviour* Penguin Books, 1972.

imagination and less sensitivity can breeze into an interview without a care in the world, and experienced interviewers would probably be more than a little suspicious of them because the impression is that they are not taking the interview seriously.

However, an excess of nerves can seriously undermine your ability to respond actively and effectively to the questions, so here are a few reminders to help you:

- The interview belongs to you. It is your chance to show yourself off, so take it.
- You have nothing to lose. Even if you do not get the job or you do not sell your product, you are no worse off than before the interview.
- You have done your preparation and have decided on what points you want to put across, so forget about yourself and concentrate your attention on the interviewer and the interview.
- Interviewers are often as nervous as interviewees. Part of your task is to reassure them that you can be trusted to handle your part efficiently.
- And a piece of practical advice: Check where the interview is being conducted and allow plenty of time to get there, so that there are no last-minute panics.

Here are also a few words of caution.

- Alcohol is of limited use. It deadens nerves but, at the same time, fuddles the brain. Drinking also shows. You can disguise the smell, but it is virtually impossible to camouflage the heightened colour of the cheeks or to improve the slurred speech, both of which any sharp-eyed interviewer will spot immediately. And I am not talking about intoxication. Even a small amount of alcohol will have this effect.
- Tranquillisers are not much better. They, too, can help you achieve some degree of calm, but only by sacrificing alertness. Both tranquillisers and alcohol, of course, are also

potentially habit-forming, with all the additional difficulties that brings. No interview is worth that!

- If you sweat when you are nervous, be prepared to deal with the problem, because, like it or not, people tend to react negatively towards the clammy handshake, the sodden garment, the damp forehead. Bathing, and clean, well-laundered clothes are an essential part of good preparation. Make sure you have a tissue to dry your hands on before you go into the interview room.

- Combat negative thoughts. Shy people tend to have more of them than most, but even those who are not normally unsure of themselves can be suddenly assailed by self-doubt before something as important as an interview. Remind yourself that you would not be going to the interview unless you had been invited.

- Do not let anyone else try to undermine your confidence. I always make a point of avoiding pessimists before crucial events, because negative thinking is like a virus and if you are in their company for too long, you will be affected by their own self-doubts.

PROJECTING YOURSELF THROUGH POSITIVE BODY LANGUAGE

In the previous chapter we saw how through body language – that complex vocabulary of posture, gesture and expressions, of voice and eyes – we express our inner thoughts and feelings. Animals use body language to regulate their entire social life – competing, mating, rearing children and cooperating in groups. Humans use it only slightly less. At least 50 per cent of all our interpersonal communication depends on body language. As has been said: 'We speak with our voices but we converse with our whole bodies.'

An understanding of body language aids you in two ways. First, if you are aware of what you are doing, you can control the signals you are sending to ensure that you are conveying the correct message; and second, you can observe and understand what others are telling you through their body language.

We have already seen how you can help create rapport by rewarding interviewees with the knowledge that they are doing a good job. Now we will look at how your body language can help you project a positive image, and what the interviewer's body language tells you about your own performance. The key thought to keep in mind is that you can control your body language to say what you want to say about yourself.

Once again I must add a note of warning: individual movements on their own mean little. Only when they form part of a consistent pattern do they carry any significant meaning. You scratch your leg because it itches, but if you also bite your bottom lip, fidget and breath rapidly, the chances are that you are very tense.

Controlling your body

Prepare yourself well before the interview – when you get up in the morning, or even, if you have had a restless night, at dawn when your resistance is low and negative thoughts invade your peace of mind. Take a few moments to think yourself into the interview. See yourself sitting with your interviewer and imagine yourself as you would like your interviewer to see you – not crushed by self-doubt, but self-assured and purposeful. Fix on that image and do not let it go until you are in the interview, when it will transform itself into reality.

Choose your clothes to suit the positive image you wish to project. Like your voice, they should not shout your worth (nor need they hide it), but convey it in a businesslike but interesting manner. Always dress appropriately, and keep in mind how you would like your interviewer to remember you, since first impressions are lasting impressions. Make your dress decisions the night before, when you have more time and can attend to those annoying little repairs that always seem to demand attention at the last minute.

On the day itself, unless you have nerves of steel, you are bound to feel some anxiety. Do not try to fight it – use it. Make it work for you by turning into the adrenalin necessary to give you that extra charge that will help you give your best performance. In case of emergency, a simple but effective antidote, I have found, is deep breathing. While sitting in the waiting room, inhale slowly from the diaphragm as singers do, not from the top of the chest, and slowly exhale. By concentrating all your thoughts on doing this elementary physical act correctly, you tend to forget the nagging doubts summoned up by the ordeal ahead of you.

- Having finally made it to the interview, enter the room in a brisk, confident manner. If you are wearing a jacket, unbutton it, because the open jacket indicates that mentally you are open and ready to engage in a fruitful discussion. However, be guided by appearance in this instance. Double-breasted suit jackets, for instance, can flap about and look untidy.
- Look the interviewer in the eye, not down at your feet or at some distant point. Sit down in the chair offered to you with your posterior well into the back of the seat, not on the edge, otherwise you may look as though you are hoping to make a quick get-away.
- Lean slightly forward towards the interviewer. By doing so, you are giving out the clear signal that you are keen to participate in what is about to happen.
- Cross your legs, but only if you find this posture comfortable. Women tend to cross theirs at the ankles, men at the knees. Remember that you are half-way towards taking up a defensive stance, so do not cross your arms as well.
- Keep your head up. If you lower it, you will be unable to maintain good eye contact with the interviewer, and your voice will be muffled.
- Square your shoulders, but do not take up the rigid posture of a small, frightened child before the dreaded headteacher, though you may, in fact, feel like one. The hunched position conveys fear and withdrawal.

- Avoid touching your face. Scratching your nose, rubbing your eyes, feeling the back of your collar are all signs of tension. They can also signal that you do not fully believe what you are saying, or indeed, that you are not telling the truth. Policemen will confirm that, during an interrogation, they watch out for the nose-scratching gesture as an indication that the suspect is lying.

- Hands, if left to themselves, are veritable chatterboxes, so keep them under control at all times. As you sit down, rest them comfortably in your lap or on the arms of the chair. If you clench them, wring them or grip your chair or your arms tightly, the interviewer can rightly assume that you are under tremendous stress.

- Keeping control of your hands does not mean sitting like a dummy. It is perfectly natural and desirable to use them to emphasise a point or to show enthusiasm; but, when you make a gesture, do so boldly. A half-lifted hand is a sign of indecision. Do not wave them about unless you want to distract the interviewer from what you are saying.

- Cupping or stroking your chin or pressing a finger to your cheek and tilting your head slightly shows that you are listening with intense concentration, which is good news to the interviewer who will respond by reacting positively towards you.

- When they feel relatively at ease with each other, people start unconsciously to mirror each other's body language. This is normally a sign that rapport has been established. If, therefore, you wish to convey this message to your interviewers, you can *consciously* imitate their movements, but do so with great care because, if they sense that you are doing it deliberately, they may conclude that you are making fun of them, and that will turn them against you.

Controlling facial expressions

We look at faces more than any other part of people's bodies. They give us more information than we are getting in words. If they indicate by their expression that they like us, we tend as a rule to feel positive towards them; and similarly if they show dislike, we, in turn, reject them.

We learn from infancy how to control our expressions to a remarkable degree to obtain the things we want – food, or the warmth of our mother's arms, and we carry that knowledge into adulthood. The English language recognises this fact by referring to our 'private' and our 'public' faces; the first, only we and our mirrors see; the latter, we display to the world and change according to the company we are in. Card players, for whom the wrong expression can mean the loss of thousands, are not called 'poker-faced' for nothing.

● Our eyebrows are rather less easy to control, as they respond rapidly to stimuli. They also have their own vocabulary, ranging from the high position indicating shock and disbelief, through expressions of surprise (half-raised), puzzlement (half-lowered) and anger (fully lowered).

● We are drawn to people who smile at us, and put off by those who look at us coldly and indifferently so, if you want the interviewer to react positively towards you in those vital first four minutes, go into the interview with a natural smile on your face that reflects your sincere desire to like and to be liked. The smile, however, must be a genuine one. A false grin will be immediately obvious to the perceptive interviewer.

● It is important that you adopt a positive expression for another reason: our expressions reflect our feelings; but equally, our emotions follow our expressions. Therefore, if we go about with the clear eye and friendly expression of a happy, confident individual, we feel it.

● Never suggest by your expression that you think the interviewer is conducting the interview badly. Even when you are convinced that you can do the job better, control your urge to frown, purse your lips or tighten your jaw muscles, since these are clear signs of disapproval which, unless they are blind or totally self-absorbed, interviewers are bound to notice. Exercising tact and patience, as we shall see below, is a far better way of helping interviewers to improve their performance.

Controlling eye contact

A famous Japanese Sumo wrestler on a recent visit to London said, 'The eyes of my opponent tell me more than any words. If I look at his eyes, I know if I can win.'

The best source of information about how we are interacting with other people is through our eyes. As with smiling, we learn the importance of eye contact in our early infancy. From about one month, babies start to watch their mother's face with increased alertness while feeding. They also react positively to receiving eye contact from her, and are distressed if they do not.

We look at other people far more than we realise – anything between 30 per cent and 70 per cent of the time, and if we are particularly interested in them, we may look at them almost continuously. Two people in love can gaze at each other for hours, and though hardly a word passes between them, they are in complete harmony.

In interviewing, where the interest quotient is also unusually high, much of the unspoken yet vital interaction that takes place is governed by what our eyes are saying. From the nature and direction of our eye contact, we can tell when it is our turn to speak and when to stay silent, how much to say and sometimes even what to say. If, in response to a reply, an interviewer opens her eyes wide in surprise, the interviewee may rightly judge that it was not the one expected and may accordingly amend it.

This leads to consequences of great importance for interviewees which affect their legitimate aim to win approval.

● Establish eye contact immediately you meet interviewers, as it is the most effective way to make them notice you.

- The more you look at them during the course of the interview, the more they will think you like them and, in turn, will think positively of you.

- Looking is rewarding, so always look at interviewers when they are speaking because, by doing so, you are telling them that you are interested in what they have to say.

- Look at them when they ask you a question. Averting your glance makes you look furtive, as though you have something to hide.

- Men should look at male interviewers and women at female interviewers about 60–70 per cent of the time; but the amount is about 10 per cent lower if the genders of interviewer and interviewee are different.

- We look more often when we listen than when we speak. When you want to break off looking at the interviewers, do so downwards, not upwards or sideways because that makes it appear as though you have suddenly lost all interest in them. Some years ago I was invited to appear on a prerecorded television 'chat-show' to talk about a new book of mine. The interviewer was professional, if not exactly warm. But what I most remember was that, while we were saying goodbye, his next guest came up behind me. He turned and as his eyes focused on the guest, it was as though I had ceased to exist. It was an unnerving experience and, instead of thinking well of the interviewer, I was left with a distinct impression of his phoniness and insincerity.

- Eye contact, though steady, should never be so intense that interviewers feel you are trying either to dominate or intimidate them. Staring fixedly at them may also convey the suggestion that you want to become friendlier with them than the circumstances warrant, which can be particularly embarrassing if they are of the opposite sex.

- In a panel or board recruitment interview, maintain eye contact with whoever is questioning you, but when replying glance at the others to include them in your answer. Experienced teachers and speakers can keep a large audience engrossed by ensuring that their eyes settle on everyone for a couple of seconds as if to say, 'Don't worry, I haven't forgotten you.'

Controlling your voice

For some reason, people tend to take their voices for granted and forget how important they can be in projecting their personalities. The voice is a flexible instrument and can be easily adapted to keep others interested in what we are saying.

As with body language, the voice is a useful guide to emotions. It is possible to 'read' an emotional state, not only by what is said, but also by the way it is said. We know angry people shout, though sometimes, if they are trying hard to control their anger, they speak in exaggeratedly low, quiet voices. Nervous people tend to speak quickly and at a higher pitch. Depressed people speak softly and at a slow pace.

Trained interviewers listen to interviewees' voices to assess their feelings, irrespective of what they are saying. An appraisee may tell her appraiser that she is happy in her present job and that she gets on well with her colleagues, but she clears her throat repeatedly and speaks quietly with a slight tremor. Added to that, her eyes are turned downwards and her hands clench and unclench. Together, the message she is conveying is directly opposite to what she is saying.

Interviewees should be allowed to speak about 80 per cent of the time, though this varies according to the nature of the interview and to the style of the interviewer. A doctor interviewing a patient may have to speak more frequently than a lawyer interviewing a client, because the doctor has to supply a lot of information in order to obtain correct answers on which to base a diagnosis, whereas the lawyer's questions should set off the client and all that is required of the lawyer is to guide the progress of the interview.

Here are a few hints to get more out of your voice:

- Open your mouth when you speak. If you cannot be

heard, the interviewer may ask you to repeat yourself once or even twice, but after that will probably cease caring what you are saying.

- Do not cover your mouth with your hand. Apart from being inaudible, you are sending out the message that you are reluctant to tell interviewers all you know.

- Enunciate your words clearly. As Greville Janner says rather severely in his book on presentation, 'Slovenly enunciation is like careless dress – discourteous and unacceptable.'[3]

- Give yourself a chance to settle into the interview by speaking more slowly at the start. This gives you a chance to consider what you are saying more carefully and for the interviewer to become accustomed to your speech patterns. It takes some interviewers a minute or two to do this, especially if they have been interviewing a number of people within a short period. You can always speed up your replies as the interview progresses and you become more confident.

- Regional or national accents are irrelevant so long as what you are saying can be clearly understood. In fact, an accent can sometimes be an advantage. The 'halo effect' (q.v.) may work in an interviewee's favour if the interviewer happens to come from the same region.

- Use the whole range of your voice. Most of us have a far greater range than we think, but often because of shyness, limit ourselves to one. A monotonous drone can drive the most patient interviewer to distraction, and a dull, lifeless voice is also an indication of a pedestrian mind, one that sees the world as flat and colourless.

- Avoid, if possible, the upper ranges, because the higher the pitch, the more nervous and uncertain you sound.

- Deeper voices carry more conviction. Fair or not, that is the view of most interviewers — shared, I might add, by producers of radio and television commercials who, for this reason, tend to use more men than women for 'voice-overs'.

---

[3] *Janner on Presentation*, Business Books Ltd (1989).

- Even though you are enthusiastic, keep your voice steady. Gushing or squeaking with excitement makes you sound silly and out of control.
- The more confident you are, the more control you have over your voice, and as has been said frequently before, the better prepared you are, the more confident you will be.
- Reduce 'Ums' and 'Ers' to a minimum, otherwise you will sound hesitant and unsure of yourself. Taken to an extreme, they make it hard for interviewers to follow your line of thought.
- If you are not certain of what to say, you can delay your reply with phrases like, 'That's a very interesting question', or the old standby, 'I'm glad you asked me that'. One to put a glow of self-satisfaction on the interviewer's face is, 'I've never been asked that before', or the modest admission, 'That's a hard one! I'll need a couple of seconds to think about it.'
- You can use your voice to 'reward' interviewers in other ways, as, for instance, when they are talking to accompany your approving nods with remarks such as, 'How interesting!', 'I never thought of that!', 'Really!', and so on.
- If you think it would increase the impact you have on others – particularly if you have to be interviewed frequently in your line of work – you might consider some voice training. A few inexpensive lessons with a voice coach can make all the difference.

To sum up: interviewers pick up messages from the way we act and the way we speak that may confirm or contradict the words we speak. They can detect hostility, boredom, irritation, frustration, worry, as well as pleasure, enthusiasm, calm, friendliness, interest, confidence and a whole host of emotions. Furthermore, without realising it, the messages we send can make a profound difference between what we feel within us and how we are perceived by others. And how we are perceived may make the difference between achieving our purpose – the job we are after, a favourable appraisal leading to promotion or rise, the sale of our product – or not.

It would be a sad world if we had to monitor every word we uttered and every gesture we made, because we would lose all spontaneity, and with that would go the essence that makes us what we are. The key is to strike a balance between being aware of yourself and being too self-conscious. Listen to your body. Teach yourself how to control it to make the impression you want – then forget about it. That way, you will achieve your goal.

THE ART OF GOOD LISTENING

Before analysing what is good listening, let us briefly look at what may be called 'false' listening, or 'going through the motions', as in the following:

- gazing at the interviewer with apparently rapt attention, but thinking of something else
- staring at a point to the side of the interviewer's right ear, and thinking of nothing
- nodding your head, murmuring encouraging phrases like, 'Yes, how interesting', but thinking exactly the opposite
- staring at your feet or picking fluff off your clothes, and thinking of what you want to say next
- waiting until the interviewer has finished, before asking a question on an entirely unrelated subject
- *not* waiting for the interviewer to finish talking before asking a question

Good listening is more than merely registering that someone has spoken to you. It is an active creative process that involves:

- hearing the feelings that lie behind the words
- hearing what people do not say but can be understood from their body language
- hearing what they actually say, not what you want them to say

- being tolerant of their foibles and their mannerisms, of which you may not approve

It demands the following qualities:

Participation

Good listeners do not merely sit back and take in information. By your gestures and your expressions you show that you are involved in what the interviewer is saying. You comment on their remarks when appropriate and ask questions in order to keep the flow of conversation moving at a brisk and lively pace.

Concentration

We are talking here about total involvement – the ability to give your mind over entirely to what is happening in the present and putting all other thoughts out of your mind. It means cutting yourself off mentally from the world outside the relationship you have temporarily formed with the interviewer. It means thinking consciously of what the interviewer is saying, not of other questions or comments you wish to make when they have finished speaking. Watch a practised politician on television respond to a question, and you will see that no matter what the situation – the economy is in a state of terminal collapse, the world is on the brink of war – their attention is riveted entirely on the presenter.

Empathy

Why should the ability to put yourself in another person's shoes improve your listening skills? The answer is that, in an ideal world all interviewers would be interesting and lively, keeping you alert and amused and at the same time challenging you with good, clear, unambiguous questions. They would start on time, finish on time, and run the interview at a crisp pace. You would not be bored by long speeches, nor would you have to wait through awkward pauses while they thought of the next question to ask. Alas, as we shall see in the next chapter, such paragons do not exist. Like most interviewees, they are far from perfect. As a good listener you should make allowances for their imperfections, and try not to teach them their business; you have enough to do as it is. Be patient. Showing impatience by either gesture or expression only makes matters worse. Maintain your poise, answer them as fully as possible, no matter how poor their questions, and discreetly but firmly guide the interview in the direction that would best help you. Also, if you are aware of their feelings, you can also use all the skills at your disposal to create a friendly relationship so that they warm to you and give you *their* full attention when *you* speak.

Objectivity

First impressions count with interviewees just as much as with interviewers. Interviewees, being human, are just as likely to pass negative judgements on interviewers after a few minutes' acquaintance, and to base these on interviewers' mannerisms and accents without giving them much chance to prove themselves. Open-minded interviewees will suspend judgement for as long as possible, and will listen with care and attention to what interviewers have to say before either approving of them or condemning them.

Listening in an active and creative way does not come naturally; it takes practice to develop the skill. Unfortunately, for the reasons discussed below, we do not always listen properly, with the result that we answer questions wrongly and make inaccurate assessments of how we are being received by the interviewers.

These are the **blocks to good listening**:

Tension

Mark walks into the interview for his annual appraisal. He wanted to prepare himself better, but somehow did not find the time. The firm has been declaring redundancies every other week, and as Mark has had some problems since moving into his new department, he is expecting to be told the worse.

His personnel officer puts her first question in a friendly manner: 'How are you enjoying working in accounts?'

Because he is so tense, Mark does not hear her question, but something completely different.

'I don't know what you've been told,' he counters, 'but none of it's true.'

Now, of course, the personnel officer is alerted to possible problems and starts to probe more deeply to find out what is making him so worried, and the whole nature of the appraisal changes, possibly to Mark's disadvantage.

Tension is infectious, and the inexperienced interviewer will become equally anxious when faced with a worried interviewee, so that neither will listen properly to the other. They will miss those subtle inflections, the particular choice of words, the pauses and hesitations that give statements and remarks their full meaning. Worse still, like Mark, they may hear what they fear most – not what was said.

Bias

None of us is free of bias. We all carry around with us views, opinions and attitudes based to some extent on prejudice. Your interviewer may speak in a high-pitched, timid voice which reminds you of someone you dislike, or have some other mannerism that irritates you, with the result that you are only half-interested in what he says and you miss the significance of some of his questions. Your answers, therefore, go only half-way to providing him with the information he is seeking, and he will judge you accordingly.

To be a good listener – and therefore a good interviewee – you must first recognise your bias and then leave it outside the interview room. Clear your mind and listen to what the interviewer is asking you, otherwise you will not give the right answers.

Preoccupation

Sonia's first novel had just come out and her publishers were keen that she gave an interview to a prominent magazine. Just before she met the journalist, her agent had rung to tell her the good news that a film producer had expressed interest in turning the novel into a movie; however, to counter that, she was having difficulties raising money to buy a house. These events – good and bad – were in her mind, so that she gave brief, superficial replies to all the questions put to her. Her chance of making an impact on the public as a young writer with plenty to say had been lost; in fact, the journalist made her out to be an awkward and unresponsive individual whose achievement was probably no more than a flash in the pan.

We listen four times faster than we talk. Do not waste that time thinking about matters about which you can do nothing for the present, but use it to evaluate what is being communicated and to anticipate your next contribution. Interviews seldom last long, and while you are engaged in one, enter it fully with body and mind. You can resume the rest of your life, with its triumphs and failures, its problems and its achievements, the moment the interview is over.

FACE YOUR NEXT INTERVIEW

Verbosity

'The reason why I talk so much,' George Bernard Shaw once boasted, 'is not to have to listen to what other people say.'

That may have been fine for Shaw, who was not only world famous as a dramatist and writer, but was totally convinced of his own genius. However, it is not an attitude generally to be recommended to ordinary interviewees, who have to project themselves and establish their identity in the minds of the interviewers.

Like Shaw, many people treat interviews as an opportunity to make speeches (in the old newsreels of him, he beams with unadulterated pleasure when responding to journalists' questions). The trouble is that few have his wit. Others cannot bear silences and have to talk continually, otherwise they feel they are not making sufficient impression on the interviewer.

Rather than filling up the time interviewers give you with empty rhetoric, encourage them to speak, because not only will this help to win them over, but you might also learn from them. After all, you know what you are going to say; you do not know what useful information you may receive.

Impatience

Robert came well-prepared for his interview for a new job. He learnt all he could about the company and about the job itself; he had also done some useful reading about the nature of the work he would have to do if he got the job, and he read every book on interviewing he could lay his hands on, learning replies to possible questions off by heart. Now he was ready to give of his best.

Unfortunately, so eager was he that he hardly gave the recruiter a chance to ask a question before interrupting with a reply:

Interviewer: 'Described the kind of boss you – '

106

Robert: 'Most like to work for? That's easy. Someone who is loyal to – '

Interviewer: 'I was going to say, "least liked", but no matter, carry on.'

The interviewer let the first one pass, but when it happened again, she was forced to ask Robert to wait until she had finished speaking before replying. Eventually he realised that if he continued to interrupt, he would ruin the interview and lose his chance of being offered the job.

Impatience is like a bolting horse; the more freedom you give it, the greater the danger that it will lead you into ground full of potholes and overhanging branches that might unseat you. Take your time. You will have your chance to make your points; but if you let your eagerness get the better of you, you will anticipate interviewers' questions and will misinterpret what they want to know. You could also inadvertently give away more information than you need to, and end up with nothing to show for your effort.

CHECKLIST

- Keep your answers brief, and when you have said all you have to say, stop talking.
- Listen carefully not only to the question itself, but also to the additional information being supplied by body language and facial expressions.
- Establish a good rapport with the interviewer, as it will make communication between you easier.
- Empathisc with nervous and inexperienced interviewers, and help them where possible by asking questions.
- Show interviewers you are interested in what they are saying by your body language and expressions.
- Do not interrupt, even if they are taking a long while to make their point.
- Do not attempt to put words into their mouths.
- Do not argue with them. Interviews are not debates.

'READING' THE INTERVIEWERS' BODY LANGUAGE

Interviewers are not in the business of giving interviewees guidance and training in interviewing skills. They will not help you to answer their questions, nor will they tell you how well or badly you are doing – not consciously, at least. However, if you are sensitive to their non-verbal communication, you can judge your performance by the way they behave.

What, in the main, you are looking for are signs that the interviewer is listening to you and approves of, or is giving serious weight to, what you are saying, in which case you will continue more or less as you are doing. But you may see other signs – of boredom, irritation, and disapproval – which will tell you to change or vary your performance.

Approval – 'I've taken to you immediately and I'm interested in everything you say'

Listeners who are interested in what they are being told tend to sit in a relaxed and comfortable posture. If they move at all, it will be to lean toward you. Their faces will be lifted up so that they can maintain eye contact with you all the time you are speaking, and they will nod their head from time to time while uttering encouraging phrases such as, 'How interesting', 'I never realised that'. They will also respond immediately to what you are saying with the appropriate expressions. They may, without realising it, start to mirror your body language, so that when you cross your legs, they will cross theirs, when you lean back, they will, too.

These positive signs will tell you that you are handling yourself and the questions well, and that you should continue in this way. However, be careful not to become complacent. Pride goes before a fall and an unexpected question may throw you completely, or you may forfeit the important element of self-control and blurt out something that spoils everything you have said before.

Evaluation – 'I haven't made up my mind about you yet'
This suspension of judgement is reflected in a number of ways. They tilt their heads or prop them up in the manner of Rodin's famous statue, The Thinker. Their index finger is pressed against the side of the nose, or they hold a finger to their lips. Chin and beard-stroking is a common evaluation gesture. If they wear glasses, they may look over them in a quizzical way, as if to say, 'I'm not sure I follow you', and by sucking the tip of the spectacle frame or pressing it against their lips, they are indicating that they are not prepared to say anything until they have heard more. If they lower their heads, close their eyes, and pinch the top of their nose it means they really cannot make up their minds.

Should you observe any of these gestures, you may have to accept that you have not yet made your case and you may have to change your approach if you want to convince the interviewer.

Interruption – 'If only you'd stop talking for a moment, I might get a word in edgeways'.
Trained interviewers will abide by the principle that interviews belong to interviewees, that they are the focal point to which interviewers should give their full attention, and that they should be allowed to speak up to 80 per cent of the time. That is why they will ask open questions which motivate interviewees to respond fully, and will encourage them by using the appropriate body language. Sometimes interviewees are so carried away by their own eloquence that they ignore the interviewer's attempts to stop them, and turn the interview into a monologue, taking each question as an opportunity to make a speech. They even talk over questions.

Be on guard for signals that warn you of the interviewer's desire to interrupt and contribute something to the discussion. It will probably start with a hand or only a finger lifted tentatively, but if this is ignored, the signs become bolder: tugging the earlobe, clearing the throat, fidgeting. If all else fails, the interviewer will break into your monologue with another question, or with a summary of what you have said so far. They may also try to distract you. In desperation they may use all three strategies: first, reassuring you by saying, 'That's very interesting.' Then distracting you, 'But I'd like to come back to that a little later on.' Finally, asking you another questions, 'But now I'd like to know why . . .'.

This is not a cue for you to go into a sulk, only a reminder that interviews are a two-way process and that you are there to gain information, as much as to impart it.

Boredom – 'This must be the most tedious story I have ever heard. Will it never end?'

Signs of boredom are difficult to disguise. Look around you when you are next sitting in your dentist's waiting-room or in an airport lounge, and you will quickly identify the unmistakable clusters of gesture and expression.

Here are some of the more obvious:

- Loss of eye contact is your first warning that something is wrong; but even if you are being looked at, it does not mean that you are being *seen*. The unblinking stare can be just as much of a danger signal as drooping eyes. However, when the interviewer's eyes close, then you know that emergency measures must be taken.
- The hands clench and unclench, the fingers intertwine, drum on the table, click the top of a ball-point pen, or, *in extremis*, doodle. In a recruitment interview, it will be on your application form or CV.
- The feet perform a dance on the floor, tapping silently to a rhythm only they can hear, or they will gently kick the desk.
- Well-mannered interviewers try to maintain an interested pose, so you may not be able to read too much in it, but if they rest their head in their hand, as though it has become too heavy to hold, then you are in trouble!

If you see *any* of these signs, your first step is to stop talking. This will bring the interviewer up sharply and the ensuing silence will demand that another question be asked so that the interview can continue. But you have been given a warning not to go back to your old ways.

CHECKLIST

- Think of the interview and not yourself.
- Talk about subjects which are interesting to the inter- viewers as well as yourself.
- Keep your responses short and to the point.
- Know when you have said all you have to say, and stop!
- Maintain good eye contact with those you are talking to.
- Be animated in your facial expressions.
- Use the full range of your voice (tone, rhythm, volume) to convey your message.
- Concentrate on what the interviewer is saying to you.
- Listen, and show it by your facial expression and your posture.
- Do not be afraid to make your point.
- Agree with the interviewers because you believe in what they are saying, not merely to conform.
- Do not be afraid to express opinions (without hurting other people's feelings).
- Do not take yourself too seriously. Aim to be poised, without being pompous.
- Smile when appropriate, which does not mean all the time.
- Be serious when appropriate, which does not mean all the time.
- Do not work too hard at being liked.

5

TERMINATION

COPING WITH BAD AND INCOMPETENT INTERVIEWERS

Interviews, to be challenging and rewarding, need to be a real encounter, a meeting of two minds engaged in the pursuit of information for the same purpose. Those that are too relaxed and easy-going are usually devoid of genuine interest, and the amount of useful information that passes is limited. For this reason, it is common for 'easy' interviews to be followed by more difficult ones, which makes the first wasteful of time and effort.

There is a difference between encounter and confrontation. In the former, the participants are stretched to their fullest by the mutual exchange of question and answer; in the latter, they face each other as adversaries. Only in the former is real rapport and proper communication established and the original purpose realised.

Most interviewers fall between the permissive, who lie back, as it were, and let interviewees walk over them, and dictators, who force their will on interviewees to make them behave as they wish them to. The best interviewers are those who know what information is important and use all their skills to get it. It is not their task to make life simple for interviewees, but to obtain the information they need. Interviewees are perfectly entitled to keep back information that they believe is irrelevant to the purpose – and the best do so without destroying rapport – but interviewers have to go behind the evasions, half-truths,

112

clichés, asides and lies and get to the truth, or as close to it as possible.

Interviewees are entitled to expect that:

- they will be courteously received, fairly treated and taken seriously
- the interview will be conducted in a room that is both convenient and quiet, where they will not be interrupted, and that the seating arrangements will help to create a friendly and relaxed atmosphere
- the interview will start and finish on time and that the interviewer will be properly prepared so as to know what questions to ask
- they will not be bored
- the interviewer will not only make them think, but give them ample opportunity to reply in full.

What of the interviewers themselves? Interviewees are entitled to expect that they should be:

- self-disciplined and self-controlled
- friendly, but not excessively so
- in possession of empathy
- objective
- in possession of mental and physical poise
- trustworthy

They do not want interviewers to assume the mantle of judge and jury, nor do they wish them to be doctors or psychologists who interfere with their private lives on the pretext of trying to help them solve their problems. Whatever their attitudes towards people outside the interview-room, inside the interview-room interviewers should be free of prejudice and listen to what interviewees have to say, without registering signs of censure or disapproval.

A tall order, you might say, that few can fill, and you would be right. The fact is, you are much more likely to meet, and to have to cope with, flawed individuals whose lack of basic interviewing skills beggars description.

As with all interpersonal skills, some people are naturally better at interviewing than others; but everyone can be taught, and can improve with practice. The problem is that so many interviewers believe themselves to be naturally gifted and in no need of training, and so few companies provide them with the opportunity to change their attitude.

I would like, now, to introduce you to some interviewers you may come across if you are especially unfortunate. I do so not to frighten you, but to prepare you so that you will know how to deal with their particular failings and emerge from the interview with your dignity and self-esteem intact. These characters are, I might add, in no particular order of ghastliness. You may, incidentally, recognise some of them as counterparts of the awful interviewees described earlier in the chapter on rapport.

Amateurs

They will always be with us, because they believe that interviewing comes naturally and that everyone can do it. No one is perfect, but they are even less perfect than most. You will recognise them from their blank stare, which tells you they are not sure who you are or why they are interviewing you. When you remind them, they will not be fazed, but will trust to those tried and true instincts that somehow have got them through many an awkward interview unscathed. They will have done no preparation and will be unclear as to the purpose of the interview. Lacking method or organisation, they will proceed in a disjointed way, jumping from subject to subject, losing you in the process. Not having been worked out in advance, their questions will be mainly closed, and if the amateur is recruiting you, the answers to most of them would be found in your CV or application form, if only they had thought of consulting it beforehand:

Interviewer: 'So you went to university?'
Interviewee: 'Yes.'
Interviewer: 'And you studied electronics?'
Interviewee: 'Yes.'
Interviewer: 'You didn't get a First, I see.'
Interviewee: 'No.'
And so on . . .

Amateurs waste time, but if you have prepared yourself properly, their incompetence can be your passport to fame and fortune, since you can direct the interview where you want to go and drive home the points you wish to make.

Some years ago after I had published a book, a reporter was sent by the local newspaper to interview me. Her opening remarks are etched on my memory as evidence of the archetypal amateur at work. 'I'm sorry, I don't know anything about you and I've not read your book,' she began as she entered the room, 'but my editor sent me to get some information for a feature.'

After my initial irritation had passed, I gave her a glowing account of my life which she repeated in the feature almost word for word.

Babblers

Their questions go on forever; then, just as you start to reply, they interrupt with another one, or a long comment on the previous answer. At recruitment interviews, they are so keen on selling you their own brilliance, the wonderful job, or their amazing organisation that they are not interested in listening to what you have to offer. When you do finally get a chance to speak, their eyes glaze over with boredom, or become fixed on a point behind your shoulder, so that, you soon start to wonder what you are doing there. They, too, are terrible time-wasters and unless you make a move to finish the interview, they will go on for as long as it suits them.

The best way to interrupt the flow is by asking questions relevant to the subject of the interview:

Interviewer: 'You'll realise, of course, that even if we allow you to do some extra training, you will still have to remain in your present department though I know you are keen to move on, but you see, at the moment, we can't really afford to give you a promotion because . . .'

Interviewee: 'When do you think you can move me on?'

Interviewer: 'Well, that's what I've been trying to tell you. You see – '

Interviewee: 'Shall we say in three months?'

If that method does not work, there is always the excuse of another appointment: 'I'm sorry, I'll have to go. I'm seeing the MD in half-an-hour. Do you think we could move on?'

Candidates may have to suffer the tedium if they want the job badly enough; but they must remember that they may be working for the Babbler and will have to put up with their interminable monologues for a long time.

Policemen

Some famous media interviewers fall into this category, and though their programmes can be enjoyable – who does not relish the sight of a pompous and self-serving politician squirming – they should not be regarded by interviewers as role models. Policemen resemble Bullies (see below) in their enjoyment of power for power's sake, but they differ in that they keep strictly to the rules of interviewing and forswear the use of unfair tactics. They treat you either as a lowly subordinate or a criminal. They will greet you and shake your hand firmly, but you will not feel welcome.

Interviews with them are soulless and uncreative. Little rapport is established, most of their questions are closed and they do not expect or require you to expand on your replies. They do not like you asking too many questions, because they like to be in control all the time and they have worked out a

116

rigid plan in advance which your questions threaten to disturb. If you try to develop a point, they will interrupt with a curt, 'Please, just answer my question', as though they were in a court of law.

They also, when inclined, resort to leading questions:

Interviewer: 'You play sport, don't you?'

Interviewee: 'Yes, a little.'

Interviewer: 'Team sports, I take it.'

Interviewee: 'Not really. It's squash.'

Interviewer: 'I see. Well, we are a team-led company, you know.'

They also sit in judgement, letting you know by the frown, the pursed lips or shake of head that they believe nothing you tell them. They never agree with you, but they are too well-trained actually to argue.

Appraising you, they remember every little peccadillo you have committed or which has been reported to them since the last interview, and they condemn you before you have a chance to defend yourself, making you feel that you are not worth the money they pay you.

Your choice with Policemen is either to play the part of the accused, in which case you will find yourself explaining or excusing all your actions, or to refuse. If you acknowledge that you are not perfect but refuse to defend yourself for every single act in your career, they have to back down:

Appraiser: 'Why did you let the problem develop? You should've dealt with Bob's complaint. He was a valuable man to lose.

Interviewee: 'I sent you a full report at the time, giving both sides of the argument. If it's mislaid, I'll be happy to send you another copy.'

Appraiser: 'I haven't had time to read it. Let's move on.'

Bullies

A species of Policeman. Perhaps troubled by a deep-seated sense of inadequacy, they like to make interviewees feel small.

They do not bother to put you at ease by getting up to shake your hand, but either sit in silence behind their desk (for self-protection) or gesture to the single chair facing them. They prefer the confrontational face-to-face approach because it enables them to stare you down more easily. Sitting at a comfortable angle to interviewees smacks of empathy or rapport, neither of which they believe in.

Their questions are usually closed, or if open, invariable start with 'Why'.

'Why have your grades been consistently so low?'

'Why do you say you were never consulted?'

'Why did you not achieve more in your last job?'

'Why do you want this job?'

Journalists conduct entire interviews without giving the interviewee a chance to answer a single question fully, as in a recent interview I heard:

Reporter: 'Minister, your department intends to spend £20 million for development of underwater equipment for the Navy. In light of the current recession, wouldn't you say this was a wasteful use of scarce funds?'

Minister: 'It is my opinion – '

Reporter: 'Please answer my question. Yes or No?'

Minister: 'I wish to make my position clear – '

Reporter: 'Minister, you're obviously not keen to give a straight answer, so I'll move on to another question.'

Minister(by now completely beaten): 'I'm perfectly happy to answer – .'

Bullies have to be dealt with in interviews as they are in life – they have to be resisted. Candidates can end the interview and walk out. But in the workplace, subordinates do not have that option. Nevertheless, they can refuse to be intimidated. They can pick the right time and ask – not demand – why they are being 'got at'. Managers sometimes do not realise they are acting the Bully and are surprised when you point it out to them; and as long as you are polite and do not allow them to anger you, you can sometimes persuade them to change their approach.

Fidgets

As their name implies, Fidgets cannot remain still for long. They pace up and down the room while you are trying to reply to their questions, and if they remain seated, they constantly move about as though their chair were hot. They play with objects on their desk (of which they always seem to have an ample supply); they make little balls out of paper – your CV – (I know one who also used to chew the paper); and they bite their nails, examining their handiwork from time to time. They cannot maintain eye contact for long; their eyes roam the room as though searching for an escape, and, even more distracting, they glance repeatedly at their watches.

Their brains fidget as much as their bodies. They leap about from subject to subject, making it impossible for interviewees to concentrate. After a few minutes spent in their company they will exhaust you, so it is important for you to *summarise* whenever possible.

Summarising is a very useful tool to employ whenever the interview loses its place. Summaries are signposts which help you to see where you have come from and where you are going to. If the interview is going off the track, summaries help to put it back on again. They should, however, be kept short and to the point. If they go on too long, they break the flow.

When you think the time is right, you will say something like, 'I'm sorry, but I seem to have lost the point. Could we go back a bit?', then proceed to give a summary of what has been said during the last few minutes. This should force the interviewer to concentrate on the direction of the interview and get it going again with another relevant question.

Fidgets probably do not intend it, but the effect of their impatience is to unsettle interviewees and make them feel unimportant. So, to preserve your sanity, you have to stay calm and, by your body language and facial expressions, let them know that you will continue to keep your wits about you and answer their questions as best you can, no matter how muddled and disorderly their own minds are.

Jokers

They read somewhere that the best way to make inteviewees feel at ease was to tell them jokes. This is wrong. The way to put interviewees at ease is to greet them in a friendly manner and to get on with the interview as speedily and efficiently as possible. But Jokers are either so anxious themselves, or so lacking in empathy, that they do not realise that the result of their thoughtless witticisms is to make their interviewees feel distinctly uncomfortable and embarrassed. They also fail to understand that their flippancy implies that the interview or interviewee is not to be taken seriously.

Many years ago when I was, for a (thankfully) brief period an assistant headteacher, a pupil came to me in tears because one of her teachers to whom she had gone to discuss her future career had flippantly remarked, 'Well, if all else fails, you can always be a bricklayer.'

He was not normally a thoughtless man, and when I confronted him about the remark he was genuinely surprised and upset that she had taken it seriously, as he had not intended it to be. 'I was only trying to cheer her up,' he explained. I had to point out that if he had possessed a little more empathy, he would have understood the depth of her anxiety, and that making a feeble joke was not the way to calm her fears about her future.

The other problem with Jokers is that their humour is not always in good taste. They joke about interviewees' names if they are at all unusual ('That's quite a tongue-twister!'). They tease young interviewees with references to their looks or age ('You don't look old enough to be out of school, let alone applying for a senior post like this!'). Women, in particular, are made to squirm at their facetious comments ('What's a pretty girl like you doing applying for an engineer's job?').

Unless their 'jokes' are actually insulting or demeaning or, in the last example, in contravention of the Equal Opportunities legislation, it is not a good idea to overreact. They are usually unaware of the effect of their attempts at humour, and if you

120

make a fuss they are likely to become hostile and the interview will be jeopardised. If, however, you are applying for a job and will have to work with the Joker, you may decide you would rather end the interview and leave; but if he or, less often, she, is someone you would prefer to maintain contact with, you can point out tactfully – by not laughing every time – that you do not find their remarks amusing.

Jokers, we are told, are the life and soul of parties, but interviews are not parties and Jokers can do a great deal of damage to interviewees who do not have the strength of mind either to ignore them or to let them know that they are stepping out of bounds.

Don Juans

Invariably men, though women have also been known to abuse their power in a similar manner, they imagine they are irresistible to the opposite sex, and they treat every interview as a potential sexual encounter. They are seldom so obvious as to lay themselves open to a charge of harassment, but everything they do or say reveals them to be basically contemptuous of women.

Their demeanour is over-familiar and flirtatious. Their handshake lingers and is sometimes accompanied by a hand on the arm or back. Their eye contact, instead of being friendly and intermittent, is persistent. They have arranged the chairs so that they are sitting well within touching distance, and may take the opportunity to emphasise a point by the light pat on the knee or shoulder.

As a general point about personal space, we are, each of us, acutely aware of how much of it we prefer about us. This is our portable domain that we carry about with us, which we adjust according to who we are with. We do not mind being close to someone we love; in fact, we prefer it. We keep casual acquaintances about three to five feet away from us, and interviewers, or anyone else in business situations, from four to twelve feet distant. This applies more to Northern Europe and North America. In other parts of the world – Africa or Asia – personal space is less significant and strangers or acquaintances who keep the same distances could be seen as aloof and unfriendly.

If a Don Juan invades your space with the clear intention of imposing himself on you in an unacceptable way, simply move your chair further back; if a hand does finds its way on to your knee, either stare at it fixedly until it is removed, or push it away. On no account permit it to remain where it is out of fear or politeness, because the Don Juan will take this as encouragement and proceed to the next stage of seduction.

Because their status gives them power, few of their victims have the courage to complain, so they continue with their odious activities undetected. This is regrettable, and should you be in the unfortunate position of having to fend off their attentions, do not hesitate to report them to their superiors. One complaint may be ignored; repeated complaints may force them to take action.

Shoulders

Shoulders confuse sympathy with empathy. Empathy is putting oneself in the position of others so as to understand how they feel; sympathy is suffering with them. There is, of course, place for both in our lives; but interviewers should remain as objective as possible.

Shoulders are always there for you to lean or cry on, if you need them, and even though you might only wish to give them information, they encourage you to express your feelings by their expression, by shaking their heads and murmuring sympathetic phrases like, 'How awful it must've been for you', 'How unfortunate', 'How brave you were.'

Some interviewers use sympathy as an exercise of power, but in a more subtle and, possibly, more dangerous way than Bullies. They do not insult you or hurt your feelings, but they want you to become dependent on them, and in so doing undermine your self-respect. Do not encourage them to do so by treating them as confessors or confidants.

These examples of bad or incompetent interviewers are, admittedly, exaggerated, but only slightly. Though few fall clearly into any one category, most are tainted by one or more of these unfortunate traits. Nice though it would be to assure you that you will escape the worst of them, the truth is that, as there are far more untrained interviewers than trained, far more inexperienced than experienced, far more closed than open-minded, the chances are high that you will come across one or more of them in your career. Awareness of these interviewers and their problems is half the battle; the other half is knowing your own worth and ensuring that, no matter how incompetent they are, you make them aware of it, too.

COPING WITH STRESS

We all go about with an idea of who we are, our *self-image*. We know our name, our sex and age, how we feel and how we look. We also have an attitude towards this self-image. We may like it some of the time and not at others; we may like it a great deal or not very much. Most of us also have an image in mind of what we would like to be, and the more closely we resemble that ideal, the more stable we are as individuals. The greater the conflict between ourselves and our ideal, the less stable we are.

Our self-esteem, feeling good about ourselves, is a very valuable part of our personal equipment. With too little of it, we are wretched. For interviewees with a stable sense of themselves, the stress interview, though unpleasant, will not do them much harm; but for those with inadequate self-esteem, it can wreak havoc with their self-image, causing them untold misery long after the interview has finished. And for what?

Some interviewers believe stress interviewing to be the most effective way of making interviewees reveal more about themselves than they might otherwise have done, that by destroying their self-esteem they strip them bare of all pretensions, defences and deceptions. Thus stripped bare, so the theory goes, they can be seen as they really are, not as they would like the interviewer to see them.

Another theory is that stress interviewing tests the interviewee's ability to handle stress at work. But does it? Certainly, it tells the interviewer how well the interviewee handles the pressure of the interview, but can that information be applied to how they will behave in the real-life situation, where the circumstances of their job will be governed by completely different and more complex demands? I suggest it cannot.

You might gather from what I have said that I have little time for this technique. This is not to say that interviewers should make their interviews undemanding. On the contrary, they have a duty to make them as tough as they can, but they can achieve this far more effectively by being polite and businesslike, by asking interesting questions that make interviewees think, by giving them the freedom to respond fully, and by letting them leave the interview with their dignity and sense of self-worth intact.

How to recognise a stress interview

You can do this the moment you enter the interview room, which will probably be bare of most signs of human activity. You will be greeted in a cursory, off-hand manner; no one will shake your hand, and there will be no small talk to put you at your ease. The interviewer will sit behind a desk in a chair larger and possibly higher than yours, with arms, whereas there will be nowhere for you to rest your hands. Your chair may also be placed some distance from the desk, to force you to speak louder and at the same time to strain in order to hear what the interviewer is saying. It is also possible that you will be facing a window, the glare from which will cause you discomfort.

The interviewer's tone of voice will be flat, or tinged with hostility. Eye contact will be minimal. His or her posture will indicate superiority or indifference: hands behind the back of the head, legs crossed, head facing away from you; then, occasionally, just to confuse you, the interviewer will lean forward, hands steepled in front of face to stare at you accusingly.

No attempt will be made to establish rapport with you; the interviewer will remain aloof and cold, the stern Parent with the terrified, helpless Child. Questions will be closed, designed not to challenge, but to belittle. Your attempts at giving detailed replies will be received with sighs of boredom, yawns, ostentatious glances at the wristwatch or the clock on the desk. The interviewer's face will remain expressionless throughout, to make you feel inadequate, unimportant and insecure.

Other stress techniques

- The repeated use of the question, 'Why?' to anger you and make you lose control.

Interviewer: 'Why did you leave university before obtaining your degree?'

Interviewee: 'I'd run out of money.'

Interviewer: 'Why?'

Interviewee: 'My expenses were higher than I anticipated.'

Interviewer: 'Why was that?' (And so on, *ad nauseam*.)

- Blow hot, blow cold – or, Mr/Ms Nice, Mr/Ms Nasty.
The interviewer changes unexpectedly from being warm and approachable to being distant and cool, to confuse and unnerve you. When there are two interviewers, this technique is even more effective, as police forces all around the world have discovered. You may be welcomed by one in a normal, friendly fashion, then, just as you are settling down to enjoy the interview, the other hurls hostile questions at you, pressing you to reply and interrupting you when you are doing so. Then

the first interviewer comes back with an easy question. So it goes on until, thrown repeatedly off course, you are reduced to a twitching wreck.

- Silence

Interviewing is not all talk; silences have an important part to play. They occur, for instance, when interviewers run out of questions or lose their way, in which case it is perfectly proper for interviewees to say nothing until the interviewer finds their way again. Interviewers legitimately use silence to encourage interviewees to give fuller replies to their questions. Here, they wait expectantly, to let the interviewee know that there is more to be said. Other than perhaps causing a little discomfort for the interviewee, no harm is done, and it may be that the additional information supplied is to the interviewee's advantage.

Silence when your reply is perfectly adequate is used deliberately to unsettle you and throw you into confusion. You believe you have replied in full, but the interviewer says nothing and stares, either directly at you, or at some other point in the room until you start to feel uncomfortable. You try hesitantly to add to what you have already said, only to find that your attempts are treated in the same way. Whatever you do, you cannot win. If you stay silent, you give the impression you are hiding something and are therefore guilty of deception; if you speak, or rather stammer, you are equally guilty, but now of muddleheadedness.

How to cope with stress interviews

- Keep calm and composed. Try not to let the interviewer fluster you.
- Even if you feel angry or bewildered, do not allow your feelings to show. Sit comfortably with your legs and arms uncrossed; keep your hands away from your face and rest them in front of you, preferably with palms outwards to show openness.

126

- Do not let the interviewer rush you; take your time to consider your replies before you give them.
- If you do not understand the question or the information the interviewer wants, do not be afraid to ask, e.g. 'I'm not sure what you had in mind when you asked that question. Perhaps you could explain?'
- Avoid the trap set for you by leading questions, the purpose of which is to make you feel at fault, which can be very effective in breaking down your self-confidence. A question such as, 'What are your main weaknesses?' implies that you have many. You can reply, 'No one is perfect, but if I really thought that my weaknesses would affect the way I do the job, I wouldn't have applied for it.' Or you can roll back the question by asking, 'What do you mean by "weaknesses"?'
- Maintain regular eye contact. If you look nervously back and forth, the interviewer will know that you are mentally 'on the run' and you will be pursued until you are cornered. Then one big bite, and it's all over!
- Do not try to stare down the interviewer. You will probably not win, and even if you do, the victory will be an empty one because the interviewer will resent you for the humiliation. Stress interviews are very much about power, so it is best to let them know subtly that they have not won, without pointing up their failure.
- Do not excuse or explain yourself, because the interviewer will regard this as a victory:

Interviewer: 'You seem to have changed jobs quite frequently. Why?'

Interviewee: 'Is that how it appears to you? I thought of it as gaining and broadening my experience.' (*Not*: 'Well, circumstances seemed to be against me. First there was the recession, then I had to commute a long distance; then I had to take a cut in salary and couldn't afford it.')

- Do not break a silence by adding to your answer more than you think it deserves. The additional information will either be irrelevant, or may reveal more than you intended.

Remain calm, do not fidget or show signs of discomfort and either wait for the interviewer to speak, glancing up expectantly from time to time or ask, 'Is there anything more you want to know?'

- Once you have made your point, but have received no acknowledgement from the interviewer, do not go back on it. It will make you sound as though you are admitting that you are in some way at fault:

Interviewer: 'Why did you achieve so little in your last job?'

Interviewee: 'I think I did pretty well, all things considered. I got on well with most of the people there, and I managed to bring in some very useful new practices.'

Silence.

'I find it difficult to think what more I could've done. But in the job before that where I had more scope, I also . . .' (then proceed to make some very effective points about your past achievements).

Not: 'Well, I suppose I might've done better if I'd stayed longer . . .'.

- Finally, remember the old saying: *This, too, shall pass.* Even if you are having a bad time, the interview will not last forever. You will soon be out of the room, so, with courage and persistence, make the most of it while you are there.

If none of the above suggestions works and the interviewer persists in trying to break you down, you may have to consider seriously whether you want the interview to continue. You are a free agent and it is within your power to end it at any time. A young colleague of mine was once subjected to the kind of treatment we have just discussed, which ended finally when the interviewer asked him why he had told him so many lies during the interview. As he knew he had not, he challenged the interviewer to admit that he was using stress techniques. The interviewer laughingly agreed, adding, 'And because you've seen through me, I believe you're the man I'm looking for.' 'Thank you,' said my colleague, 'but I'd rather not work for you.' With that, he got up and left, regretting only that he had not done so sooner.

ENDING THE INTERVIEW IN YOUR FAVOUR

Some general hints

The timing and manner – the when and how – of terminating the interview tend usually to be at the behest of the interviewer, not the interviewee, and they usually signpost the end by summarising what you have told them up till then and by asking you if you have any questions you would like to ask. This is your opportunity to deal with any area of the subject that has either not been covered at all or, in your opinion, not sufficiently.

You should have already thought up some key questions as part of your preparation, but more may occur to you during the interview, which is why it is a good idea always to have a pad and pen with you. Not only do they make you look proficient and businesslike, but you can jot down any thoughts or questions, so as not to forget them. Do not, however, ask unnecessary and irrelevant questions merely to fill up time or to make conversation. Interviewers have probably worked out in advance how long they can give to each interview and, if they are considerate people, they will not want to cut you short, but by prolonging the interview unnecessarily, you leave them no alternative. (See Part Two, Checklist 1 for questions candidates can ask at the end of a recruitment interview.)

Do not assume the interview has ended until the interviewer makes it clear that it has, otherwise you may find yourself in the situation of Sue, one of my journalism students, who had been interviewed by a Sunday newspaper for a feature on 'turning forty'. After they had talked for twenty minutes or so on general subjects, the journalist turned off the tape recorder and began asking more intimate questions about Sue's private life. How was she managing as a single woman again after recently being divorced? 'Oh,' Sue said with a twinkle in her eye, 'I do all right, especially since I realised how much I like younger men.'

When the article came out, it concentrated, not surprisingly except to Sue, almost exclusively on her relationships with younger men. At first she was annoyed and felt she had been betrayed; but in discussion with the class, she agreed that the journalist had not misreported her, nor had she said at any point that the interview was over. Sue had merely assumed it was when the journalist switched off the tape recorder.

Remember: last impressions linger longest. If you want to be sure that they are favourable, fix in your mind the picture of yourself that you would want the interviewer to keep, and concentrate your energies on achieving it.

For this purpose:

• Take your leave as quickly and politely as possible. Interviewers will thank you for it.
• Interviewers lacking confidence frequently end in an awkward and unbusinesslike manner. It is not your responsibility to relieve them of discomfort, so avoid making off-the-cuff remarks to fill in embarrassing silences.
• Do not add any afterthoughts. If the subject matter is important, you should have mentioned it during the interview; it is no excuse to say that you were not asked the appropriate questions, because you should have found the opportunity to give the information anyway. By adding it at the end, you diminish its importance and convey the impression that it is you, and not the interviewer, who is disorganised.
• No matter what has gone on during the interview, do not leave in a huff. Try as far as possible to resolve any outstanding conflicts and uncertainties that might still exist between you and the interviewer.

Beware of interviewers who use their final questions in order to trap you into making admissions or revealing confidential information. Interviewing, to many, is an arduous and stressful experience – even to those who are used to being in the public eye. The relief that comes when things are starting to wind down is often so great that they start to relax. As we saw with Sue, not until you and the interviewer have parted company are you entitled to feel safe. Until then, remain in control of your material or yourself.

Where possible, get in the last word:

Reporter: 'Isn't it a fact that you have already decided to shut half the junior schools in the borough?'

Local politician: 'What? Where did you – ?'

Reporter: 'And that you are sacking 250 teachers?'

Local politician: 'I have never, I repeat never – '.

Reporter: 'There, I'm afraid, we must leave it, but I'm sure our readers will be very interested in what you have just told me.'

If, instead of blustering, the politician had been more alert, he would have come straight back with a denial: 'These are all lies concocted by the opposition . . .', which would have put an immediate stop to that line of questioning and, by adding, 'It is clear that they are jealous of our success because they know perfectly well that their own policies are in a complete mess!', making a small but useful attack on the other party.

- End on a confident, optimistic note. None of us knows what the future will bring. The result of the interview may be success or failure. But trying to prejudge it at this stage is pointless, and may leave you feeling dejected. Keep these feelings to yourself.
- Let your body language tell the interviewer that you valued the interview. Do not come slowly to your feet as though you are carrying the world on your shoulders, but stand up briskly. Maintain eye contact because, if you look away or down, it sends a message that you feel embarrassed by your performance.
- Shake your interviewer's hand, if offered to you, and smile. Thank them for giving their time, although it may be your time they have taken up. Small courtesies cost nothing.

6

UNFINISHED BUSINESS

Interviews are an integral part of modern life and are impossible to avoid. They occur in our work – applying for a job, improving our status or salary, selling, negotiating; they occur in our private and domestic lives, when we consult our doctor, accountant, lawyer and bank manager. Yet, unless we are in a job where it is essential that we are proficient in the skill, we are unlikely ever to receive any training in how to be good interviewees.

I believe that employees *should* receive training, because they would make better interviewees and consequently the interviews with their superiors would be more efficient; but I know this idea is not generally shared by managers, who see interviewing as a contest which they do not wish to lose to someone better at it than they are.

TAKING NOTES

Without proper training, the best way to learn how to become a skilled interviewee is to learn from your own experience. By analysing your interviews after the event, you can see where you need to improve, and so gradually develop the necessary skills to make a capable and effective interviewee. One of the problems with self-evaluation is remembering what occurred in the interview. You cannot properly decide whether or not you handled questions well unless you can recall what you were asked and what you replied.

For most of us this is difficult to do without some form of record. We are usually so involved in what is happening and so preoccupied with doing our best that we forget what interchanges actually took place. Short-term memories are notoriously unreliable. A few gifted people have total recall, but most of us forget much of what we see and hear within a very short time. Our memories are also distorted by bias. We tend to remember only what we want to. If, therefore, we take a dislike to our interviewer, or feel we did not perform well, we will forget much of what went on, except perhaps the most embarrassing details, which will remain in our minds for years. However, if we liked the interviewer and thought we did well, we will remember everything far more clearly.

Interviewers also have this problem, but they solve it by taking notes or recordings of the interview. Is it permissible for interviewees to follow their example?

A lot depends on who you are. Certain senior politicians and business tycoons insist that all their interviews are recorded, to obviate the danger of being misquoted; but the rest of us do not possess the clout to impose such conditions.

Can a candidate at a selection interview, for instance, take notes of what has transpired?

If you are a senior manager applying for a job, there may be a number of important facts about, say, the financial position of the company you are thinking of joining that you need to know before you can make your decision, and rather than try to keep them in your head, it would be regarded as right and proper for you to note them down.

On the other hand, if you are applying as a school-leaver for a junior post, the interviewer might think it somewhat laughable or pretentious if you asked permission to jot down notes during the course of the interview. However, when it comes to the final stage when you ask the questions, the situation is different and interviewers would consider you efficient and well-organised if you took notes of their replies.

The answer whether or not to take notes depends on the circumstances and the context of the interview, and whether you can make them without disrupting or disturbing the proceedings.

If you write slowly and have to break eye contact, you will interrupt the flow of the interview and inhibit the rapport built up between you and the interviewer. And if you cannot transcribe your notes because they are illegible, you might as well leave your pad and pen behind.

CHECKLIST

- Always ask the interviewer's permission to make notes.
- If, for whatever reason, permission is not granted, make them as soon after the interview as possible.
- Keep them short. Put down only the points that you may need to refer to later.
- Keep a record of all the awkward questions you were asked, and your replies as far as you can remember them. Referred to later, you will be able to improve on them where necessary, or, if you thought they were correct, learn them for next time.
- Facts are easier to record than feelings, but you should, where possible, try to put down what you felt about the questions as well as the replies you gave. Note also the interviewer's reactions.
- Do not make the notes while you are still emotionally upset from the interview. They will be distorted by your feelings and will not accurately reflect what actually took place. Wait until you are calmer before putting down your thoughts.
- Keep your notes in a safe place (e.g. with application forms and CVs) so that you can refer to them to refresh your memory before your next interview.
- Compare your previous notes to those made more recently, to see how well your interviewing skills are progressing.

SELF-EVALUATION

An interview is far too arduous and time-consuming to be entered into carelessly, so before you do so, ask yourself the simple question: what's in it for me?

If it is a job, you should seriously consider whether this is a job you want, whether it fits into your present career plans, whether you believe you are properly suited for it, and what you can bring to the organisation which is advertising the job. If it is an increase in salary or a promotion, why you think this is the right time to ask for it and what chances you think you have of success.

If you have been contacted by, or have made contact with, the media to talk about a product or service you are offering to the public, ask yourself whether this is the right time for the interview. The timing of promotional interviews is crucial. Too often they are conducted well before the product is launched so that, by the time it is on the market, people have forgotten everything that was said about it. You should also ask yourself whether you are the right person for the interview, or whether there is someone else in your organisation better equipped to answer the questions. Finally, ask whether the interview is worthwhile. It is gratifying to one's ego to be asked to go on a radio programme, but you may find that you have to travel to far-flung parts of the country for an interview lasting no more than five minutes – and at your own expense!

By this stage of the process you may know that the purpose of the interview has or has not been achieved, but your work is not finished, because you are about to start on the final but most important part of the process – preparing yourself for your next interview through self-evaluation.

Interviewing has been described as an art, but that implies that it cannot be learnt – you can either do it or you cannot. I prefer to regard it as a craft – one that with practice can be continually improved on.

Each interview we attend is a learning experience. We gain information not only about our interviewers, but, more importantly, about ourselves. Fear, the inability to relate to others, lack of emotional stability, immaturity – these exist in all of us to a greater or lesser degree, but through our experience we can learn how to overcome our weaknesses and reinforce our strengths so that, with time, we become more effective at presenting ourselves to others.

When Robert Burns wrote, 'O wad some Pow'r the giftie gi'e us, To see oursel's as other see us', he might have been thinking of interviewees. It is notoriously difficult to know how we come across to interviewers. The interviewee who was convinced he was witty and charming and that his answers were scintillating would be mortified to learn that his interviewer thought he was arrogant and tedious. The interviewee who thought she failed completely to put herself over would be astonished to hear that her interviewer thought she was pleasantly modest in her demeanour and that her replies were clear and to the point.

If you want to improve your skills as an interviewee, it is essential that you try to put yourself in the interviewers' shoes and see yourself as they see you. The closer your perceptions match theirs, the more accurate is your self-evaluation. As it is unlikely that you will ever know how they reacted to you except through their unconscious body language, here, following the PQRSTU System, are twenty direct questions to ask yourself to help you rate your last performance.

Preparation
- Was I well prepared for the interview?
- If the interview was on my own premises, had I prepared the room properly so as to ensure comfort, quiet and lack of disruptions?
- If the interview was for the media, did I find out who it was aimed at and how it was to be used?
- Did I dress appropriately for the interview?
- Was I punctual for my appointment?

Questions

- Did I listen carefully to the questions and make sure I understood them before I replied?
- Did I work out in advance the points I wanted to make?
- Did I anticipate the most difficult questions I might be asked, and prepare my answers?
- Were my replies brief but relevant?
- Did I deal adequately with probing questions?
- Did I handle poor questions (e.g. closed, leading, multiple) well, by giving the answers *I* wanted to give, not what the interviewer wanted me to give?

Rapport

- Did I greet the interviewer in a relaxed and friendly manner?
- Did I appear to the interviewer as a mature, confident interviewee, no matter how nervous I might have been feeling?
- Did I, through my body language and eye contact, make the interviewer aware that I felt positive towards him/her?

Skills

- Did I take the initiative and volunteer information when given the chance?
- Did I capture and hold the interviewer's attention by talking about subjects that were interesting to them as well as myself?
- Did I maintain good eye contact with the interviewer and use the full range of my voice to convey my message?

Termination

- Did I remain calm and unflustered, no matter how the interviewer tried to throw me off balance?
- Am I satisfied that I said all I had to say?
- Did I end on a confident, optimistic note?

With self-evaluation, there is no point in cheating, because you are only cheating yourself. As has been stressed, interviewing for both participants is a skill that can be learnt, and the only way to improve on a skill is to practise it with the benefit of hindsight. It must be emphasised that the exercise is not to make you feel badly about yourself. On the contrary, it is to ask yourself what you did that could have been improved on, and what you did well that you can be sure to repeat next time. Remember: the more you know about yourself, the better equipped you are to present yourself to others.

OVERCOMING DISAPPOINTMENT

Interviews are such a complex and artificial process that for all of them to go well would require a miracle, and there are not many of those about. No matter how thoroughly you prepare yourself, how sincere and forthcoming you are, not all interviews will turn out as you hope or expect.

Disappointment is an essential part of living, the other side of anticipation, and the only way to avoid it is to do nothing. If you are courageous enough to go out into the world and take chances, to make an effort in the hope that something good will come of it, you are bound occasionally to suffer failure and feel rejected. Unpleasant though the feelings are, they do have one small, but useful function: they can be seen as a corrective to unrealistic expectations.

Let us say, for example, that you apply for a job which, had you thought about it more carefully, you would have realised was beyond your present capabilities. You get an interview which, in your view, went well. By now you have convinced yourself that you can do the job and ought to get it. You do not and, of course, you are dejected. However, when you think about it more calmly, you realise that had you been accepted, you would have had serious problems coping with the responsibilities, and, in the end, would either have made yourself ill trying to keep up with its demands or would have failed miserably and been sacked.

Writers who convince themselves that they are the new Dickens are bound to suffer disappointment when their novels manage to sell only a couple of thousand copies. If they are sensible, they will accept that they are not the genius Dickens was, nor will they be as successful; but this should not stop them struggling to write the kind of novels they are capable of and enjoying whatever success they manage to achieve.

How you deal with disappointment depends to a large extent on your general attitude towards life. Some people believe that, when things go wrong, they are to blame ('I didn't get the job because I'm not any good'). They also believe that their lives will never change ('I'll never get a job I like') and that every wrong event affects every other aspect of their lives ('I didn't get that job so I won't ever be able to hold up my head again'). Their pessimistic approach makes it more difficult for them to get over disappointments and to make further efforts to change their situation. A vicious circle results: their disappointments feed their pessimism which, in turn, feeds their reluctance to try anything new. Alternatively, it may encourage them to try the impossible, leading again to disappointments – and so on.

Others, more optimistic in their outlook, maintain that failure is not always or necessarily their own fault ('With the recession, they are taking on fewer staff'); that this setback is, in any case, temporary ('But things are likely to change quite soon'), and that only specific aspects of their lives are affected by it ('But, in the meantime, there are lots of other things I can do to keep myself busy').

The challenge then is not to avoid disappointment, but coping with it when, in the ordinary course of events, it comes. Here are some suggestions to help you:

● Deal first with your feelings, which may be of anger, emptiness, a sense of loss of control over your immediate circumstances or your life in general. Unpleasant though they may be, do not try to hide from them, because they will only find other ways of insinuating themselves.

- Do not use alcohol or other drugs to repress them. Alcohol is a stimulant in only small amounts; thereafter it becomes a depressant and, by relying on it, you may be causing worse and longer lasting problems than rejection.

- Imitate the optimists. Separate your feelings from the events. Take a deep breath and consider your situation as calmly as possible, without reproaching yourself.

- Do not compare your situation with others who you think have been more successful than you, because this will only make you bitter and less able to gather your resources together to make another attempt.

- Use the self-evaluation system (q.v.) to analyse as objectively as possible what may have gone wrong at the interview and to determine what aspects of your technique need to be improved.

- Do not try to rationalise your failure by blaming others. Many reasons may account for the fact that your interview did not go as well as you hoped and did not achieve its purpose. The job you applied for may not have suited you and there may have been better candidates, your time for promotion may not yet have come, the product that you so assiduously promoted may not be quite what the public is looking for at the moment. But blaming others or yourself only serves to paralyse your will and dampen your enthusiasm, so that you cannot get on with improving your future prospects.

- Do not immediately rush around looking for other things to do. The *I Ching*, that most elegant and ancient system of divination, has an appropriate response to life's setbacks which goes as follows: 'In such times there is a temptation to advance oneself as rapidly as possible in order to accomplish something tangible. But this enthusiasm leads only to failure and humiliation if the time for achievement has not arrived. It is wise to spare ourselves the opprobrium of failure by holding back.'

- Have more than one project on the go. This is not a contradiction of the previous suggestion. What I am recommending is what I used to tell my journalism students. Concentrating too much emotion on one project to the exclusion of all others is bound to lead to disappointment. Much better that they should have at least three articles or ideas out with different editors so that, when that inevitable brown envelope flops heavily down on their carpet with the returned submission, they can cheer themselves up with the thought that they have others out at the same time.

So it should be with all your projects. Only geniuses can afford to seek perfection in one task with single-minded determination (and even they seldom find it). The rest of us have to make do with our imperfect natures and our vague, imprecise ambitions, and pursue the best way to realise our potential, knowing that we are bound to fail from time to time, while always being prepared to try again.

PART TWO

THE PQRSTU SYSTEM IN ACTION

7

INTERVIEWING FOR A JOB

Recruitment is essentially an information-seeking process.
The task of interviewers is to obtain sufficient usable informa-
tion to assess who fits the job specification most closely. Inter-
viewees require information to decide whether the job suits
them.

PREPARATION

√   You are marketing yourself, so prepare yourself as though
you were a product or service you are selling.
√   Decide who you are in terms of the job you are seeking.
Make a list of all your relevant strengths.
√   Ask yourself how does the job fit into your life and your
long-term goals. (Your own misconceptions as to who you are
may result in finding yourself in the wrong job.)
√   Decide on the basic salary you need to meet your commitments, the salary you would most like to get, and the one you
would be happy to settle for.
√   Find out as much as you can about the organisation, its
products, services, its size, history, profitability, areas of
operation, growth, employment policy.
√   Decide not only what the job can do for you, but also what
you can offer your prospective employers.
√   Study the job advertisement again. Check that you know
what it is for and that you have the necessary qualifications to
fill it.

✓ If the company has issued further details about the job, salary, benefits and the like, make sure you have read and understood them.

✓ Find out, if you can, the selection process and method of interviewing being used, i.e. one-to-one or panel.

✓ If possible, find out what you can about the interviewers, their likes and dislikes, so that you can steer clear of controversial areas and concentrate on the congenial.

✓ Think up the questions you most dread being asked, and prepare appropriate answers.

✓ Try to get some interviewing practice by asking someone to put to you the questions you dread most and to check your replies.

✓ Study your application form or CV again to remind yourself of what you told the organisation about who you are.

✓ Decide in advance what you are going to wear and ensure that your clothes are clean and well-pressed. Be comfortable but not scruffy.

✓ Make sure you have the address of your prospective employers' place of business and a map if necessary. Check your route in advance and make sure you know how to get there.

✓ If you can, pay a visit to their place of business in advance. Having seen it, you will be more confident and you will have a distinct advantage over other candidates who are there for the first time.

✓ Don't flaunt your preparation. Be yourself and act naturally.

✓ Make sure you take with you:

* copies of your CV or application form
* the job advertisement
* any other details about the job supplied by the organisation
* any literature about the company such as brochures or publicity material
* reference letters, if any
* your list of questions
* a notepad and pen

QUESTIONS

√ Interviewers increasingly use standardised criteria by which to assess candidates. Be prepared, therefore, to answer questions on some or all of the following areas of interest to the employer:

* ★ work experience, including your last job and previous jobs
* ★ reasons for applying for this job
* ★ education and training, including your qualifications
* ★ intelligence, which includes your grasp of theoretical and abstract concepts
* ★ creativity and problem-solving
* ★ adaptability
* ★ reliability
* ★ attitude to authority and colleagues
* ★ motivations and aspirations, which include your long-term career plans
* ★ leisure interests
* ★ technical subjects related to the job

√ Listen carefully to the questions before replying and ask for them to be repeated if you do not understand them.

√ Always ensure that your answers relate directly to the questions.

√ Except for purely factual questions, try never to give simple yes/no replies, even to closed questions.

√ Wherever possible, answer in a positive way and use every opportunity to put yourself across.

√ Do not rush into your replies. Let the interviewer wait, rather than blurting out answers you may later regret.

√ Be as precise as you can in the language you use, and if you think you have been misunderstood, do not blame the interviewer.

√ Use questions to bounce back questions. If asked a general opening question, such as, 'Tell me about yourself', respond by asking what aspects the interviewer would like to know about, other than those mentioned in your CV.

✓   Concentrate on your strengths. Never volunteer information that exposes your weaknesses.

✓   You are not there to defend yourself against accusations about your behaviour, so do not apologise or excuse your past record.

✓   It is perfectly acceptable to put a favourable gloss on unfavourable aspects of your past ('I wasn't made redundant. They decided to close the department').

✓   Do not fake an answer; rather admit ignorance, but point out that this is what you are doing ('I'm afraid I don't know the answer, and I don't want to waste your time trying to bluff my way through.') You will be respected for it.

✓   Do not try to cover up potentially embarrassing circumstances. Without excusing yourself, explain them as plausibly as you can. ('It wasn't that we argued a lot. We just liked to explore as many different points of view as possible.')

Types of questions

✓   Open questions, no matter how probing, should be welcomed because they give you a chance to make more points about yourself and your suitability for the job.

✓   Multiple questions ('How much experience have you had doing business in France, and would you be happy to commute there regularly?') should be separated before replying. Ask the interviewer to do it for you ('Which question would you like me to answer first?').

✓   With leading questions ('Are you ambitious?'), follow the interviewer's lead unless you think that by doing so you are being forced into incriminating yourself or lying.

✓   To questions that pose a hypothetical situation ('What would you do if . . .?'), qualify your reply ('In the real circumstances, I'd probably have more information upon which to act, but in those you've given me I'd . . .'), or base your answers on your past experience ('In similar situations, my practice is always to . . .').

√ Trick questions should be thought about carefully before answering, and if you do not understand the interviewer's purpose in putting them, ask.

√ Personal questions relating to family background, marital status and future plans, religious or political affiliations and medical history should only be answered if you think they are relevant to the job you have applied for. If not, decline politely but firmly. If interviewers persist without giving a proper explanation for doing so, you may decide it is time to leave the interview.

RAPPORT

√ Greet interviewers with a smile: shake their hand if offered, and look them confidently in the eye.

√ Wait to be shown to your chair, then sit comfortably, leaning slightly forward.

√ Do not use first names unless you are asked, even if addressed by your own.

√ Get a feel of the interview from the way the interviewer behaves towards you and from the room. The more barren the surroundings, the tougher the interview; the more cluttered, the less well organised. A quiet, light, airy room posits a friendly but challenging interview.

√ If the interviewer engages in small talk, join in; but do not carry it on too long. Watch the interviewer carefully for the signal to stop. Keep to neutral subjects like travel and the weather.

√ During the warm-up, strive to find something that you have in common with the interviewer; if you succeed, play on it subtly, but do not rely on it.

√ Do not appear too anxious to please. It looks obsequious and insincere.

√ Don't get too wrapped up in yourself. Look outside yourself. Empathise with the interviewer and try to imagine what they are thinking and feeling.

√ Do not assume interviewers are confident and fully in control. Many are not, so if they see that you are at ease, they will also start to relax, and together you can then enjoy a good working relationship.

√ Reassure interviewers that you are interested and involved, by looking at them when they speak and when you answer their questions; but do not stare fixedly at them.

√ Concentrate on the interview and forget about whether you get the job or not. All you are after is the offer of a job.

√ If you have any doubts about yourself, do not show them. Remember, you would not be applying for the job unless you thought you stood at least an outside chance of getting it.

√ Interviewers make up their minds about interviewees within the first four minutes of your meeting them, and they do so on the basis of appearance, manner, expression and attitude, so it is vital that you give them a positive message about yourself.

√ It is your responsibility as much as the interviewer's to keep the communication flowing between you with as few pauses as possible.

√ Do not attempt to take over the interview by talking too much.

√ If you appear to be a mature and responsive adult, you will be treated as such; but if you remain passive and submissive, you may be treated as a child.

√ Taking the interview seriously does not mean taking yourself seriously. Lighten up, as they say, and smile when appropriate.

√ The spotlight is on you, so try to enjoy yourself. And remember, the interview will not last for ever.

√ Interviewers may be looking for negative aspects about you and your career; do not give them the chance. Wherever possible, present yourself in a positive light.

√ Enthusiasm is infectious – for the job, for what you have done in the past, and what you expect to do in the future. But do not overdo it, otherwise you will sound naïve or insincere.

√ Do not go into the interview expecting a battle, but be ready to resist any attempts to intimidate you.

√ Avoid letting the interview become mere question and answer; take up points the interviewer makes, and discuss them. This gives a more conversational tone to the interview.

√ Unless the interviewer says things that offend you, e.g. makes racial slurs, try to fit into their style of communication, without deliberately mimicking them.

√ The two enemies of rapport are anxiety and boredom. Focus on the subject, be calm, and be brief.

√ Do not argue or debate with your interviewers. If you disagree with them, do so tactfully. ('Yes, I see what you're getting at, but . . .', 'I understand what you mean, but . . .').

√ Do not correct interviewers unless the subject relates to your personal history ('That wasn't quite what I meant . . .').

√ Never be disdainful of interviewers, even if you think they know less than you. You may not realise it, but you will show your disdain in your body language.

√ If interviewers become over-familiar, either ignore them, in which case they will probably stop, or make it clear that you are attending the interview for the job and nothing else. If they persist, leave. You would not want to work for them anyway.

√ Never let interviewers persuade you, by threats or otherwise, to pursue your relationship outside the interview room. Respect yourself and the interviewer will respect you.

SKILLS

√ Present a confident, businesslike image by sitting comfortably, arms preferably by your side, hands resting either on the arms of the chair or on your lap.

√ Control your fears. If necessary, seek help from books and tapes on relaxation, readily available from libraries and bookshops.

√ Strike a balance between being excessively modest and over-assertive.

151

√ Remain poised throughout, no matter how much the interviewer tries to confound, bewilder, or intimidate you.

√ Share the talking. Where possible, go beyond the questions and volunteer information if you think it will help your case.

√ No matter what your true feelings are about the way the interviewer is conducting the interview, do not show them by slouching, yawning, sighing or gazing around the room.

√ Be patient with nervous and disorganised interviewers. There is no point getting annoyed or irritable with them because, like it or not, they have the whip hand.

√ Although most interviewers are not even aware of it, and would probably deny it if they were, your non-verbal behaviour – body language, facial expression, use of voice, eye contact – has a profound effect on their judgement of you. The more these convey your enthusiasm, sincerity, liking for the interviewer and total involvement in the interview, the more favourably they will view you.

√ Be open to communication by uncrossing your legs and arms, unbuttoning your jacket, and by looking up at the interviewer in a friendly receptive manner.

√ Avoid crossing your arms and hunching up your shoulders, because these gestures convey the impression that you are anxious and under great internal pressure which makes you want to block off communication.

√ Do not interrupt interviewers or attempt to put words in their mouths.

√ Avoid mirroring all the interviewer's actions and gestures. You will look like a child mimicking an adult. But the occasional copying of gesture, e.g. a smile for a smile, shows friendliness.

√ Keep an eye open for the interviewer's reactions, and if it appears that they have stopped listening to what you are saying, vary the tone of your voice or the pace of your speech; or if all that fails, fall silent. That will wake them up again.

√ Do not allow yourself to be put off from making your point if interviewers appear to be bored. Empathise with them – they might have been interviewing all day. If, however, you think you are the cause, then talk less and speed up.

√ Do not talk too loudly, and vary the speed of your delivery.

√ Use the full range of your voice, but remember that deeper voices carry more conviction.

√ Keep your hands away from your face, especially your mouth. Speak clearly and enunciate your words.

√ Avoid using words like 'I think', 'I believe'. They make you sound uncertain of yourself.

√ If interviewers fall silent after you have answered a question, this may mean that they would like more information from you, in which case they will probably look expectantly at you in a friendly manner. If you think you have more to give, add to your answer.

√ Silence may also mean interviewers are testing your ability to stand up to pressure, in which case remain calm and composed, and wait until they speak again, maintaining expectant eye contact.

√ If interviewers persist in trying to intimidate you with stress techniques, you can point out to them that you are aware of what they are doing, and why. You may add, 'I have to tell you, I am not going to let myself be intimidated.' You may not get the job, but then again you may not want to work for a firm that employs such techniques.

√ Remember, interviewers represent their organisations. If you regard them positively, you will probably feel the same about their company; equally, if you react negatively towards them, this may be because their style reflects the culture of their organisation – one you may not wish to be part of.

Listening

√ Do not talk when you should be listening.

√ Do not work out replies while you are being asked the question, otherwise you will hear only half of it. As it is, you think almost four times faster than you speak, so you will have plenty of time to hear the whole question while working out your answer.

√ Make it clear from your eye contact (steady, but not staring), facial expression (relaxed, not frowning or pursing lips), gestures (slow nodding of head) and posture (alert, leaning forward on or close to the edge of the chair) that you *are* listening to everything that is being said.

√ Do not interrupt interviewers, even if you disagree with what they are saying. Wait until they have finished talking before you make your point.

Panel interviews

All the above applies equally to panel or board interviews with some additional points, as follows:

√ The chairman of the panel is usually the one who makes the initial introductions and the final remarks. Concentrate your attention on him or her, but not to the exclusion of the others because another member of the panel may have greater influence in making final decisions.

√ Always look at the person questioning you.

√ When answering one questioner, do not ignore the others but take them in with a brief glance during the course of your answer.

√ After you have answered questions from other interviewers on the panel, turn back to the chairman.

√ Do not be put off by signals between members of the panel, because these will probably have little to do with you personally but will be about matters like time and questions still to be asked.

TERMINATION

√ The end of the interview is usually signalled by the interviewer asking you if you have any questions. It is, of course, possible that the interview has been such a full and lively exchange of information that there is nothing more to be said, in which case do not ask questions simply for the sake of doing so, it only prolongs the interview unnecessarily. Interviewing is a two-way process, and you are there to learn about the job and the company, as much as to tell them who you are. No matter how detailed their job advertisement and any further information you may have received, there will be details you need to know before you can think of accepting the offer of a job.

√ If you have prepared yourself properly for the interview, you will have made a list of questions. Some interviewers inwardly groan when you bring it out, but they will have to acknowledge that you are well organised. At the same time, do not make a meal of it. Be brief and succinct.

√ If interviewers neglect to ask you for questions, it may mean that they have genuinely forgotten or that they are testing to see whether you will assert yourself. Whatever the possible reasons, remind them politely by saying something like, 'I hope you don't mind, but there are a few points I'd like to clarify before we finish.'

Questions you can ask

About the vacancy
√ 'What happened to the last occupier of this job?' Or 'Why has the job become vacant?'
You will probably have received the answer to this during the course of the interview, but it is important that you know, because it will tell you much about the job itself, its demands, its stresses, and the people with whom you will be working if you take it. The previous employee may have left for reasons unconnected with the job, e.g. moving to another country, or they may have been promoted, in which case you will know that the company or organisation believes in rewarding its employees effectively. However, it may be that there were

significant clashes between the employee and senior members of staff, that signal possible interpersonal problems.

√ 'Have you advertised the vacancy within the organis-ation?' Or, 'Why have you not promoted someone within the organisation?'

Some organisations pride themselves on promoting staff from within, to ensure that everyone is given the incentive to improve themselves. The policy keeps everybody happy, but sacrifices dynamism. Others prefer to take in new blood, believing that that is the way to keep the organisation dyna-mic, though the result of such a policy often is a fast turnover of good people. The answer to this question may reveal the organisation's attitude towards its employees, and the more you know about them, the better your choice.

√ 'How many people have held this job in the last few years?'

√ 'How many of them are still working for the company?'

About the job itself

√ 'Could you explain where I would fit into the organisation.' If it would help, ask the interviewer to draw you a diagram of the corporate structure and your place in it.

√ 'Will I be working in a team or on my own?'

√ 'What decisions will I be able to make, and what will be outside the scope of my authority?'

√ 'Who will I have to answer to?'

√ 'What will be my immediate task?'

√ 'What will you expect of me by the end of six months?'

√ 'What promotional prospects go with the job?'

√ 'What kind of training will I get?'

√ 'How long will the training last?'

√ 'Every job has its problems, what do you foresee might be mine?'

This last question is perfectly legitimate, and it is worth prob-ing gently to get an answer. After all, you have had to talk about your weaknesses as well as your strengths so that they can assess your suitability, now it is their turn to tell you about obstacles you may have to face if you are offered the job.

About the company

Even in times of high unemployment, it is essential that you establish whether or not you would be happy working for the company. First impressions, as we have seen, are important, and you can get a good 'feel' of the atmosphere the moment you enter the premises. As a young informant told me, 'If you really like a company you present yourself a lot better in an interview. If you feel you'd be happy there, you can get this enthusiasm across, just as when you like a person – and the person likes you – you are much more enthusiastic towards them.'

It is the seemingly small details that make the difference. How you are received, the state of the waiting-room, and, of course, the treatment you receive from the interviewer – all these are clues from which you can gauge the nature of the environment in which you may be working. In addition, there are important questions you can ask which will help you confirm your impressions.

√ 'What is the management structure?'
√ 'How are decisions made here?'
√ 'How is the job performance appraised?'
√ 'What kind of support do I get?'
√ 'Am I expected to keep rigid times, or do you operate a flexitime system?'
√ 'Do you have a dress code, and if so, what is it?'

If you are going for a more senior post, you are also entitled to know something about the company's financial condition and its future potential:

√ 'What problems have you experienced in the recent downturn in business?'
√ 'Have you any problems in production or distribution?'
√ 'What plans do you have for future expansion or retrenchment?'
√ 'Have you had any cash-flow problems?'
√ 'Are there any plans for moving or changing premises that I should know about?'

Finally, you need to know:

About your Candidature

√ When will I hear the results of my application?'

You ask this because, naturally, you have other irons in the fire though, you hasten to add, this vacancy is the one you would most like to fill. It is unlikely that you will be given a decision there and then, so do not expect it. Do not force the interviewer into making a quick decision, because it may not be in your best interests. Some interviewers, more our of insecurity than malice, will insist on congratulating interviewees on their performance at the conclusion of the interview. Do not take them seriously, because you are bound to be disappointed.

√ 'How will I be informed? By letter or telephone?'

Make sure that the interviewer has your address and telephone number. It should be on your CV or application form, but it is just as well to check.

√ 'How many other applicants have you interviewed for the post'?

They may not tell you, but there is no harm in asking. It will help you to assess your statistical chances of getting the job, if nothing else.

√ 'What reservations, if any, do you have about my ability to do the job?'

This takes courage to ask, but it is a good way of finding out in advance what chance you have of getting the job. If the interviewer has decided against you, they will seize the opportunity to air their uncertainties, then at least you know more or less where you stand.

About terms

√ This is *not* the time to negotiate salary and other terms, unless you are made an offer on the spot, in which case you should react enthusiastically and say that you would like a day or so to think about the offer. You are, at this point, entitled to ask about the salary range and future salary prospects, without discussing them in detail. You will also want to know about holidays and other benefits, but again, only for information. Do not enter into any negotiations about them.

158

√   If you have not already been informed about your travelling expenses, now is the time to ask. If the amount is small, do not bother, but if you have come a long way, then you should make this point politely. You may have second thoughts about joining a company mean enough not to agree to reimburse you.

√   Obviously you cannot ask all the questions listed above, otherwise you will be conducting another interview, and many of them will have been answered in the course of the interview. Restrict your final questions to the most essential. You will have your chance to find out more if you are offered the job, or if there is a subsequent interview.

Making a good exit

√   Leave in the same polite and self-assured way you entered, by looking the interviewer in the eye, or, in the case of a panel, glancing at each member, smiling, and giving a firm handshake if offered.

√   If you are not sure of the way out of the building, ask directions. Some buildings are mazes, and interviewers forget that you have not been there before. Another staff member coming across you, a stranger, wandering about may think you are snooping.

√   A polite 'thank you' to the interviewer(s) will not go amiss, and mention that you enjoyed meeting them, but avoid embarrassing them with effusive and insincere compliments on how wonderfully interesting and inspiring the experience has been.

UNFINISHED BUSINESS

√   The anxiety of the waiting period can be greatly reduced by having more than one application 'on the go' because, while you are expecting this result, you are preparing for your next interview, which will be even better than the last because of what you have learnt from the experience.

√ You will have asked and been told how long you will have to wait for the result and in what form it will come – a letter or a telephone call; but even in the best organised office, papers go missing and there may be a delay in letting you know. There is also a possibility that the company is inefficient, thoughtless or, perish the thought, plain ill-mannered. What do you do?

√ Unless there is some degree of urgency – another offer, for example – give them a couple of weeks' grace before writing.

√ Remind them of the date of the interview and ask them politely when they think they will let you know. If the delay is longer than another month or two, you can be firmer. 'You did promise to let me know within a week and it is now nearly a month . . .'

√ If you have not succeeded in being offered the job, should you find out why, or should you get on with the next application? I incline to the latter particularly if, as a result of your self-evaluation, you acknowledge that you were not suited for the job. In my own career, I thank my lucky stars for those interviewers who knew better than I that I was not the right person for the job, because through their perspicacity I have missed what might have been some very unhappy experiences.

√ If. however, you feel that the interview was a success and that, all things being equal, the job should have been yours, then write a polite letter of enquiry, thanking the interviewer and saying that you would appreciate it if they would give you some indication of what in their view went wrong. Take great care with the tone of the letter, so that you do not sound a bad loser or that you are questioning their decision.

√ If you feel brave enough, you can telephone, but do not be surprised if the interviewer is not available and does not call you back. Once they have agreed to talk to you, do not argue with the decision or claim that you were the best candidate, but listen to what they tell you, making notes. Afterwards, thank them for their comments. You may also ask them for their advice as to what to do next, but do not push your luck.

√ You may wish to stay in contention for any future openings, in which case you should write saying how much you enjoyed the interview and that, if the opportunity arises again, would they consider you for the same or another position better suited to your abilities? The chances of this happening are fairly remote, but it is worth the try. I once applied for a job at the start of one year and was turned down on the grounds that they had already found someone to fill it. I asked the organisation to keep my name on their files and when, at the end of that year, the position was open again, they wrote telling me and I took it.

√ Should the news be good and you are offered the job, prepare yourself to start negotiating the terms of your employment (unless these have already been clearly and unambiguously set out in the original job description). Do not expect that the negotiations will be with the interviewer.

√ Work out in advance the package of salary and benefits that you would be prepared to accept. If you accept less, you must be able to justify this to yourself, otherwise you will start you new job resenting the company, and your time there will not be happy.

√ Remember the old rule, *unless you ask, you will not be given*. Within the limits of good sense, ask the salary and the benefits that you believe you are worth. You may be pleasantly surprised to find that your future employer agrees with you.

8

FACING THE MEDIA

PREPARATION

√   Find out whatever you can about the circumstances and context of the interview and, if possible, the interviewer who will interview you.

√   Find out in advance how the interview will be used: as a feature, a news story, or background material.

√   Decide whether the interview will be worthwhile in terms of time spent and publicity gained.

√   Decide whether you are the right person to be interviewed. There may be someone else in your organisation who has more time to prepare properly or is better equipped to answer the questions.

√   Research your product so that you know it thoroughly (find out what you need to know from colleagues, reading, any other source).

√   Determine what you want to get out of the interview; the main points you want to get across – not more than two or three.

√   Determine the minor points you'd also like to get across – not more than three or four.

√   Prepare some good anecdotes that you can use to illustrate the point(s) you want to make. A good story often makes your points punchier and more dramatic.

√   Good comparisons also help to explain complicated processes more readily, i.e. 'think of it [the process] as throwing a stone into a still pond and the waves it makes as . . .'.

√ Make relevant notes of possible answers (on cards or any other discreet form). This is your script that you can refer to, if necessary.

√ If the interview is on your premises, prepare the room, ensuring that it is quiet and comfortable and that you will not be disrupted.

√ Arrange the seating so that you are sitting about three to four feet away from the interviewer. A table between you is useful for cups, ashtray (see below), and tape recorder.

√ Apart from the room and seating, the same points apply to telephone interviews.

Your appearance

√ Good appearance counts for a lot. It gives your interviewer the impression that you care about yourself, and, therefore, the impression your company and product make on the public.

√ Dress comfortably so that you don't have to think about yourself, but about what you are saying. If you are going to dress in new clothes, make sure you have worn them before the interview.

√ Avoid over-bright colours, heavy jewellery, or, indeed, anything that might distract the interviewer. At the same time, you do not have to look drab.

QUESTIONS

√ Listen carefully to the questions and make sure you understand them properly before answering them. Ask for clarification if you don't understand them.

√ Avoid interrupting the interviewer or speaking over the questions.

√ Challenge any assumptions included in the question that you don't agree with (e.g. *Interviewer*: 'You are launching this product in the teeth of much criticism. Why?' *Interviewee*: 'I know of no criticisms.').

√   If asked multiple questions, ask the interviewer to separate them, otherwise you may confuse the issues.

√   If interviewers show off with jargon-loaded or mistaken questions, avoid the temptation to correct them. They'll only resent it if you make them aware of it.

√   Unless the questions relate purely to fact, don't give yes/no answers, but take the initiative and answer in full.

√   Don't ramble. Keep your answers relevant and to the point.

√   Don't use jargon, unless you are certain the interviewer understands it.

√   As far as possible, stick to the facts and leave your opinions out, unless they are the officially accepted opinions of the team and the company.

√   Seek clarification or correct the interviewer only when there is danger that he or she will misreport you or get the facts wrong.

√   Don't be afraid to use pauses before replying, before making an important statement, after an interruption and before your closing remarks.

√   If you are a team, the interviewer may try to play one of you off against the others in order to get a good story. As long as you all stick to your respective stories, they won't succeed (see below).

√   Remember, as far as the journalist is concerned, once the interview starts, everything is 'on the record'.

√   Don't let interviewers end on a disparaging note. Always get in the last word.

√   Remember: honesty is always the best publicity. If you do not know the answer, or do not want to answer, say so. Much better that than going on record with a lie. Lies ultimately get found out.

√   Never break off an interview in anger, even if you have been deliberately provoked. It leaves the impression that you have something to hide.

RAPPORT

√ First impressions are formed within the first four minutes, so make sure that they are the ones you want the interviewers to have of you.

√ Know the names of your interviewers. Write it down if your memory is bad, and be careful not to address them by the wrong name.

√ Greet interviewers with a handshake and a smile. Introduce yourself and look them in the eye when you do so. Remember that eye contact throughout the interview is vital.

√ Take a little time when meeting your interviewers to get a sense of what sort of people they are. Don't just blunder along, more concerned with your message than the person receiving it. Be aware of their body language as much as your own.

√ If appropriate, put interviewers at ease with undemanding small talk, but only if they seem uncomfortable (the weather or the traffic are good subjects).

√ Never make personal remarks to interviewers about their appearance, accent, mannerisms – even complimentary ones. They may be misunderstood.

√ On your own premises, offer tea or coffee. On the interviewer's, accept the offer unless you suffer from nerves – there's nothing like the noise of a cup and saucer in a shaky hand to reveal how you are feeling.

√ Allow the interviewer to smoke only if it does not bother you: you don't have to suffer if it does. If the interviewer lights up without asking you, this is a breech of etiquette and should be commented on politely.

√ Don't assume that you and the interviewers share common interests and attitudes, especially if they pretend that you do. That may be a trick to get you to make a careless, unconsidered and potentially self-damaging remark.

√ Flatter the interviewers, but be sincere about it. Complimenting them about their questions is the best form of flattery: 'That was an interesting question . . .', 'That's a very fair question . . .'.

√ Avoid picking arguments. If interviewers challenge a point you have made, either ignore the challenge, or acknowledge that you have differing viewpoints.

√ Remember: this is your show; the interviewers are there to help you achieve your goal, whatever that may be.

√ Assert yourself, but don't try to dominate. Aim for a mutually beneficial experience – after all, both you and the interviewer want to get something positive out of the interview.

SKILLS

√ Sit comfortably, posterior tucked well into your chair, leaning forward slightly but not slouching.

√ Give the impression that you know what is going on. Preferably keep your hands resting comfortably on your lap, and definitely away from your face.

√ Project a confident, businesslike, and authoritative image. (This has as much to do with how you present yourself as it has with how you handle the subject under discussion.)

√ If you suffer from nerves, sit quietly for a moment or so before the interview starts, and take some deep breaths. Try to do so during the interview (quietly!) as well. Shallow breathing adds to tension. Avoid alcohol or tranquillisers to calm nerves.

√ The best counter to nerves is to be well-prepared, to concentrate on the questions, the answers, and the interviewer, and not on the impression you are making.

Dealing with difficult questions

√ Remember, no one can force you to answer a question. Your aim in dealing with difficult questions is to deflect them as best you can, without appearing to do so. Here are some possible responses:

√ 'That's an important question, and to answer it I need to go into some of the background.'

√ 'I'm sorry, but I think that's a leading question. What I would like to say is . . .', *or*, 'It seems to me that you're trying to get me to agree [or to say] something . . . Would you like to tell me what it is?'

√ 'The best person/people to answer that is/are [name another person/organisation] . . .', *or*, 'I think you should ask [name another person/organisation] . . .'. (*Don't forget to tell your colleague(s) that you have given their name.*)

√ 'I'm not sure I understand the question,' (which gives you time to think up a good answer).

√ 'Why are you asking me that question?'

√ 'I don't think this is either the time or place to answer that.' *or*, 'We haven't really enough time to deal with that now in detail.'

√ 'That's a really complicated question and I need time to get all the facts together. I'd like to ring you back [or write to you] on that.' (*Remember to do so.*)

√ 'That's really not relevant, you know.' *or*, 'That's not what we're here to talk about.'

Some Do's and Don'ts

√ Don't let interviewers interrupt you until you have finished making your point, even if it means talking slightly louder and over them.

√ Know what you are talking about, but do not flaunt your knowledge.

√ If you haven't got the information at hand, don't waffle or try to bluff your way through. Admit it and assure the interviewer that you will send it on when you have it.

√ Interviewers probing for more information may ask the same question in a number of ways. Recognise what they are doing and answer them all in the same way. Eventually they'll tire of it and proceed with the interview.

√ Avoid filling silences. It's a stratagem used by interviewers to get more information than you are prepared to give, and it works only if you let it.

√ If the interviewer is deliberately trying to provoke you,

167

remain calm. Don't get into a slanging match, because it will achieve nothing.

√ Don't lecture the interviewer or lay down the law, even on your own subject.

√ Avoid any mannerisms that reveal nervousness or uncertainty, such as constantly crossing and uncrossing your legs, crossing your arms in a self-protective manner, gripping tightly on to the edge of your chair, fidgeting, scratching, and covering your mouth.

√ Use the full range of your voice to convey your message with conviction.

√ Take the interview seriously, but you don't have to be serious about yourself. On the other hand, be careful with jokes. They can misfire; so, too, can sarcasm. If you can't control the impulse to joke, aim the jokes at yourself.

TERMINATION

√ At the end of the interview, ask interviewers if you've covered everything. Don't wait for them to do it.

√ If you think it necessary, check any facts for accuracy with them.

√ Aim to leave interviewers with a favourable impression of you, your product or your organisation.

√ Paradoxically, the more you think about the impression you are making, the less impression you will make.

√ Strike a happy balance between being a faceless spokesperson and an over-eager salesperson.

√ Make interviewers feel that spending time with you has been worth their while; that they come away knowing more and feeling more positive towards you and your oganisation.

UNFINISHED BUSINESS

√ If you have promised to send interviewers any further information, make sure that you do so as soon after the interview as possible.

√   You can ask interviewers to show you a copy of the interview before it appears. They may decline to do so for fear that you will try to re-edit it. Journalists tend not to show their copy to anyone other than their editor, but they may agree to show you a transcript of the interview.

√   If it is a prior agreement that they show you their copy, then you can insist on it.

√   Ask journalists when the article is due to appear and, if possible, to send you a copy. However, don't rely on them to do so, but make sure you obtain a copy for your records.

√   If you have any complaints about the accuracy of the interview, make them as soon as possible. The longer you wait, the less impact your complaint will have.

√   Be realistic about complaints, and keep objections in proportion. Don't complain about unimportant trifles. You will appear to be petty and this can do more harm than good to your image.

√   If you liked the article, write and thank the journalist.

FACING THE INTERVIEW AS A TEAM

√   Each member must do his or her preparation. A noticeable imbalance is created if one member leaves it to the others, which the astute journalist will exploit, directing all difficult questions at those who are unprepared.

√   After you have made your individual preparations, come together to agree on the points you want to get across, the difficult questions you anticipate, and the replies you propose to give to them.

√   Your appearance as a team is important. Go for modified contrast in style and colours, rather than uniformity. You want to maintain your individuality, but at the same time give the impression that you all are one team.

√   Choose from among you one person to act as the unofficial leader who can pass questions on to those best able to deal with them.

✓   It is essential that each member handles his or her own area of expertise.

✓   Never argue or dispute with each other in front of the press.

✓   Never attack each other or make jokes about any other member of the team in public.

✓   Avoid whispering to each other in public. It looks conspiratorial.

✓   While one member of the team is answering a question, the others should listen attentively. They should never give the impression either that they have heard it all before, that they are bored, or that their own contribution is much more interesting.

✓   Team members should maintain an awareness of their body language at all times, because the trained journalist is looking out for possible dissensions and discord, which they will try to exploit.

TELEPHONE INTERVIEWS

If the journalist telephones unexpectedly, you do not have to agree to be interviewed immediately if you need time for preparation. Tell the journalist that you will call back when you are ready. *But do so*!

✓   Do not sound as though you are irritated by the interruption. If you are otherwise engaged, tell the journalist, and make another time for the interview.

✓   If the subject matter can be handled better by one of your colleagues, arrange that you will get him or her to telephone the interviewer. Again, make sure to do so, otherwise you will unnecessarily antagonise the journalist.

✓   As telephone interviews are usually shorter than face-to-face interviews, you have to make your points even more concisely.

✓   Interviewers cannot see you or how you are reacting to their questions. Equally, you cannot see them to know what they are thinking of your replies. This means that you have to use your voice to convey the impression that you want to make, and your ears to gauge their reactions.

√ While speaking, imagine you are talking to someone sitting opposite you, and project yourself in a warm and friendly manner.

√ Keep your voice steady, even if you are nervous. Sound as though you believe in yourself and what you are saying.

√ Enthusiasm is as important in telephone interviews as in any other interview. Never sound bored.

√ If you think you may be misquoted, make notes of what you are asked and how you answer.

√ If you are still not sure, write a letter confirming the points you made.

INDEX